"Charles Christian has provided the church with a long overdue resource in *Ethics in Christian Ministry*. Reading and following this prayer for the church will enrich and make healthier the ministry and mission of church leaders and the congregations they help lead."

—The Right Reverend Gregory Rickel
Eighth Episcopal Bishop of the Diocese of Olympia
The Episcopal Church in Western Washington

"My work of pastoral oversight and support provides regular evidence that lack of healthy practices can have disastrous results. Pastor Charles Christian provides a practical, yet deeply thoughtful, resource for pastors to think about and implement healthy practices. These advices are proverbial in nature; they are rooted in wisdom, not simply formulaic. Dr. Christian is working at a deeper level than fatherly advice, although these chapters are filled with love and warmth. These practices of preventative maintenance are rooted in the Bible and in careful theological reflection. I will be glad to provide this generative resource to the pastors under my oversight."

—Dr. Jeren Rowell
District Superintendent
Kansas City District Church of the Nazarene

"Having dealt all too many times with the fallout of ministerial failure, I am glad to see this book. It is timely, filled with wisdom, and very well written. I urge that this be a resource for every minister in active service and for every student in preparation for ministry. Recent news reports that the clergy is among the lowest of professions in public confidence. This is the resource needed to address the tragic stories of ministerial failure."

—Dr. Jesse C. Middendorf
General Superintendent Emeritus, Church of the Nazarene
Founding Director, Center for Pastoral Leadership, Nazarene Theological Seminary

"*Ethics in Christian Ministry* is a timely book because it understands the conflicts, opportunities, and issues faced by pastors. This book is written by a theologically astute pastor who lives where need meets grace. Pastor Christian understands the essential work of pastoral ministry and makes very practical suggestions for those engaged in parish ministry. He understands the world we occupy and charts a clear path for vital ministry in the future. This book is a must read for those entering the ministry or looking for fresh insights into the practice of ministry."

—Dr. Henry W. Spaulding II
President
Mount Vernon Nazarene University

"Pastors and other spiritual leaders want to be right. Most work at being theologically correct, but when the best of theology does not answer the need, many will 'fly by the seat of their pants.' The minister may get by with this for a while, but often the result is damaging spiritual abuse. This book by Charles Christian not only helps to identify the problem of Christian decision-making but also provides tools that will help to stretch Christian leadership toward solid practice without destroying theology. The theological principle of Christian love is found throughout the book. I highly recommend *Ethics in Christian Ministry: A Guide for Pastors and Mentors* to those who are in Christian leadership and to those who are considering being a pastor or Christian servant who guides others in their walk with Christ."

—Chaplain Bob Reagan
Thirty Years as a Senior Pastor and Twenty Years as a Healthcare Chaplain
Cameron Regional Medical Center
Cameron, Missouri

"Charles Christian's book *Ethics in Christian Ministry: A Guide for Pastors and Mentors* offers the pastor a model of preventative maintenance that is relevant to twenty-first-century Christianity and in line with God's unchanging scriptural advice. It is well structured and is a tool every pastor needs in his or her office, because it is sensitive to the peculiarities of pastoral ministry in an era when our moral compass as Christians is in a downward spiral."

—Rev. Don Cowan
Senior Pastor
First Church of the Nazarene
Fort Smith, Arkansas

"Dr. Christian has produced a masterful, much-needed work in the field of Christian ethics. From cover to cover, *Ethics in Christian Ministry* is filled with trenchant insights and relevant themes and is composed in a winsome style that is accessible to scholar and practitioner alike. This work is inviting in tone and serves as a practical resource for life in general and certainly a life in ministry. This truly is a must read for seminarians and Bible college students. I highly recommend this valuable resource."

—Rev. Dr. Jeremy Wallace
Professor of Ministry and Dean of the College
Canby Bible College
Canby, Oregon

"*Ethics in Christian Ministry* offers well-honed wisdom drawn from a life of pastoral ministry and Christian education. The author understands that what one 'purposes in the heart' requires clear practices and boundaries to stay on track. In a time when Christian ministers receive more scrutiny than ever before, it is essential that integrity be at the center of effective leadership. I will commend this book for courses in ministry ethics and pastoral leadership. Learners need not wait until a crisis arises in the field to address key markers that will sustain the vocation of ministry."

—Dr. Molly T. Marshall
President and Professor of Theology and Spiritual Formation
Central Baptist Theological Seminary
Shawnee, Kansas

"How many pastors and pastors-to-be would benefit from sage counsel provided by a senior pastor, who has excellent training in theological ethics and whose work impressively embodies the phrase 'pastoral theologian'? They are legion! I have seen students respond positively to Charles Christian's teaching. In his book, each chapter is filled with distilled wisdom for the implementation of preventative maintenance in ministry tasks, as well as theological reflection on what those tasks mean."

—Dr. Andrew Dearman
Associate Academic Dean
Fuller Theological Seminary

"What a timely book for the clergy. I love the focus on the proactive side of ministry rather than the reactive approach. The author challenges those going into the ministry to prepare well and to set the tone for ongoing ministry as they lead local churches. This is an overdue book that balances theology and everyday life. I highly encourage those with a ministerial calling to read this book first!"

—Dr. Stan Toler
Best-Selling Author and General Superintendent Emeritus
Church of the Nazarene

"Based on years of pastoral experience, Dr. Charles Christian provides theological and practical guidance on preventive maintenance in ethics, counseling, preaching, and finances. I recommend this book to those beginning in ministry and for ministry veterans."

—Dr. Mark A. Maddix
Dean, School of Theology and Christian Ministries
Northwest Nazarene University

# ETHICS IN

# CHRISTIAN

# MINISTRY

A Guide for Pastors
and Mentors

CHARLES W. CHRISTIAN

BEACON HILL PRESS
OF KANSAS CITY

Copyright 2017 by Charles W. Christian
Beacon Hill Press of Kansas City
PO Box 419527
Kansas City, MO 64141
www.BeaconHillBooks.com

ISBN 978-0-8341-3601-4

Printed in the
United States of America

Cover Design: J.R. Caines
Interior Design: Sharon Page

**Library of Congress Cataloging-in-Publication Data**
Names: Christian, Charles W., 1970- author.
Title: Ethics in Christian ministry : a guide for pastors and mentors / Charles W. Christian.
Description: Kansas City, MO : Beacon Hill Press of Kansas City, 2017. | Includes bibliographical references.
Identifiers: LCCN 2016042043 | ISBN 9780834136014 (pbk.)
Subjects: LCSH: Clergy—Professional ethics. | Christian ethics.
Classification: LCC BV4011.5 .C43 2017 | DDC 241—dc23
LC record available at https://lccn.loc.gov/2016042043

10 9 8 7 6 5 4 3 2 1

*For Edna, Jacob, and Zachary*
*Co-laborers in the gospel*

# CONTENTS

# ACKNOWLEDGMENTS

Though I have written a doctoral dissertation, over fifty articles and book reviews, and have contributed chapters to a couple of books, writing an entire book does not come easily to me. My extroverted nature consistently pulls me away from the page and toward my favorite part of pastoral work: face-to-face ministry. Therefore, many thanks are due to those who have encouraged me in this project over a period of many years—a time that included over twenty years of pastoral ministry and nearly twenty years of adjunct teaching at a variety of universities and seminaries. The churches I have served—in Texas (North Dallas), Oregon (Canby Chapel), Washington (North Seattle), Ohio (Kent), and now Missouri (Cameron)— have provided opportunities to put the key ideas of this book to the test. Parishioners have been patient with a pastor whose heart is both in the pulpit and in the academy. They have endured the mistakes I have made, often in incredibly grace-filled encounters, and in ways that have allowed me to learn and grow as a pastor. I am grateful for the church of Jesus Christ, and I am thankful that God allows me to serve in one portion of that big church, the Church of the Nazarene.

In addition to a number of encouraging parishioners, local church staff members and the men and women in local churches and on districts where I have served have also been sources of encouragement and guidance for me. I wish I had the space and memory to specifically list each one who has made an impact upon how I think about the church, theology, and ethics, but that list would comprise an entire book bigger than this one. My prayer is that this work may be a way of giving back to them and to those who will come after them. I genuinely desire to help and encourage those who are pursuing this difficult and noble calling of licensed and ordained ministry.

District and general leaders in the Church of the Nazarene have been a blessing to me as well. Many of my own leaders, including my district superintendent, Dr. Jeren Rowell, have taught me through example and through words about Christian leadership and ethics. It is always helpful to have mentors and role models, and this book is meant to make the task of both students and mentors easier. Mentors have made my life and ministry better, and I am forever grateful.

Leaders outside my own denomination have spoken into my life and ministry too. Most all of my formal academic training has been with men and women who do not belong to the same denomination as I do but who have been intentional in making sure I have been as prepared as possible to serve the church universal, the academy, and the denomination to which I happen to be called. Again, I am grateful.

My family keeps me going: they have observed me at my best and worst and yet continue to provide me with love and encouragement on this journey. My mother and father, my wife and sons, my brother, my aunts and uncles, and my grandparents (who have run their earthly race and await the Great Resurrection promised in Scripture) are a constant source of encouragement and strength. Anything good that comes from what I write, do, or say is very much a testimony to the gift my family is to me.

Universities and seminaries have allowed me to be called "professor" and to share my passion for training and interacting with students. Dallas Christian College, Nazarene Bible College, George Fox University and Seminary, Northwest Nazarene University, Warner Pacific College, European Nazarene

College, Seattle Pacific University and Seminary, Fuller Theological Seminary, Bakke Graduate University, Trinity School of Ministry, Western Seminary, Mount Vernon Nazarene University, MidAmerica Nazarene University, Wesley Seminary, Indiana Wesleyan University, and Nazarene Theological Seminary have entrusted their wonderful students to my oversight at one time or another in the past two decades. The colleagues and the students in these institutions, as well as colleagues and friends in various theological and ethics societies in which I have participated, have helped me to continually grow in the academic portion of my call to ministry. Thanks to all of you.

Bonnie Perry, René McFarland, Richard Buckner, and the editors at Beacon Hill Press of Kansas City were patient, helpful, and encouraging to me about this project from the beginning. Thanks!

This book could actually be two books: one book of my mistakes in ministry and one giving help to those who are pursuing the highest ethical concerns for ministry. This one—the one that tries to adequately introduce clergy ethics—is the shorter one! I am thankful that the big book of mistakes has been forgiven by the one to whom this book is intended to give all honor and glory. Any good that comes from this book is largely due to the way the Holy Spirit has worked through the voices of those I have alluded to above. Many of these folks have even taken time to read and reflect upon sections of this work. The shortcomings of this work are mine, but God is faithful. May all of God's people be helped and blessed by something that comes from this work.

Charles W. Christian
Cameron, Missouri
Advent 2015

# INTRODUCTION
## An Ounce of Prevention

The old sign in the mechanic's shop window read: "Pay me now . . . or pay me later." That concept applies to more than just automobiles. Preventative maintenance—paying the price up front in order to prevent higher costs later—is at the heart of maintaining health. When routine preventative maintenance—such as oil changes, fluid refills, and tire pressure checks—are neglected long enough, serious damage requiring more personal costs is the result.

No one can prepare for every crisis or emergency. The best premarital counseling simply cannot address every possible crisis in marriage. The best academic preparation cannot possibly prepare us for every crisis in any profession. Similarly, even the best-trained and most experienced Christian leader routinely encounters situations that were not covered in his or her preparatory training.[1] However, this does not negate the importance of preparation. For instance, studies show that couples who spend three to six months in premarital preparation are 80 percent less likely to divorce than those who do not. Even well-prepared engaged couples sometimes divorce. However, preventative maintenance gives them a greater opportunity for success in marriage.

The word *prevent* literally means coming before. In Wesleyan Christianity, the phrase *prevenient grace*, also called preventing grace, reminds us that the grace of God comes to us before we are aware: God takes initiative. The goal of preventative maintenance for ministry is preparation, but not in a way that seeks to take control of one's ministry. Rather, preventative maintenance involves preparing in such a way that recognizes God's prevenient grace: God is already at work, furthering his mission. We prepare for ministry in a way that recognizes this truth. For the Christian leader, up-front agreements and preparation enable us to be proactive, not simply reactive, in regard to ethical decisions. Being reactive engenders panic, which can lead to questionable ethical decisions. Proactive—not reactive—preparation for key areas of ministry often marks the difference between a successful and an unsuccessful (and brief) ministry. In ministry, just as with cars, marriages, or other professions, if we do not pay the price of preparedness up front, long-term damage results for ourselves, our families, and our ministries.

## THE PURPOSE OF THIS BOOK

The purpose of this book is to help ministers and other Christian leaders "pay now" by creating a healthy and ethical environment for ministry. The old adage states that an ounce of prevention is worth a pound of cure. While it is true that some preventative measures suggested in this book may seem like more than an "ounce" of prevention, they are less strenuous and time-consuming than the hardships and consequences that can result from neglecting these preventative measures.

Cars may break down even if the oil has been changed consistently. Married couples can go through rigorous pre-marital preparation and still feel overwhelmed at times and in need of emergency assistance. The best parenting classes cannot possibly prepare us for all of the adventures a child will put us through. Likewise, these preventative measures do not guarantee a smooth ride in every aspect of Christian ministry. Jesus himself promised that "in this world you will have trouble" (John 16:33). Ministry is dangerous. Life is dangerous. The legendary songwriter Hank Williams reminds us that we'll "never get out of this world alive!"

However, a prepared person has the tools to focus his or her best efforts upon any crises that may arise. Likewise, a prepared minister can be an example to those to whom he or she is ministering, even in the midst of the challenges and crises that come along. Preventative maintenance keeps us as prepared as possible to meet unexpected challenges. Preventative maintenance fosters healthy relationships and up-front communication, which are important investments in ourselves and in others. These investments are like a savings account that can be drawn upon when the rainy days come—and they *will* come.

This book addresses key areas of preventative maintenance in Christian ministry, including communication, relationships, preaching, counseling, and finances. My own learning from over twenty years of Christian ministry, sometimes gained the hard way, is accompanied by the wisdom of those who have ministered far better and far longer than I have. In addition, I have had the privilege of preparing Christian ministers through higher education, in university and seminary settings, for nearly twenty years. The materials I have used and the issues I have encountered among students and colleagues are added to the preventative maintenance toolbox presented here.

The chapters below set a general ethical foundation. Chapter 1 is a brief introduction to Christian approaches to ethics and ethical decision-making. Since this book focuses mainly upon the practice of ethical decision-making in ministry, chapter 1 provides only a brief introduction to the more detailed study of Christian ethics. I recommend in the citations a few more-detailed introductory texts that would be worthwhile additions to any pastor's library. Since I argue throughout the book that the identity of the Christian minister is primarily a theological one (set by God through Scripture and the church), it is important to discuss the foundations of ethics before diving into the practical outworking of our theology and ethics in the remaining chapters. This makes this book more than a simple how-to book. It is a book meant to assist ministers in setting a proper tone for their ministry: to create a healthy environment in congregations based upon the highest goals of Christian theology and ethics. There is a sense in which these chapters are useful on their own as reference guides and discussion starters, addressing the various topics included therein. However, each chapter assumes the ethical, Christ-centered foundation discussed briefly below in chapter 1. Even if you are less comfortable or familiar with academic discussions of Christian theology and ethics, chapter 1 provides a starting point that will be important in making the most out of the materials presented in this book.

## KEY AREAS OF PREVENTATIVE MAINTENANCE

With this book we will introduce or reintroduce ourselves to key areas of Christian ministry and take a proactive approach to preparing for them. This preparation includes the ability to improvise when difficult, gray areas arise. The need for improvisation in Christian ministry becomes clear rather quickly. At the beginning of my seminary studies, I was already serving as a full-time pastor, and many times I sat in class thinking, "This is very helpful, but I am going to have to adapt it a bit to my own setting." This was not an excuse to disregard the basics of ministry, biblical studies, pastoral care, and theology I was learning. Rather, it was a motivating factor for me to learn the basics so I could responsibly adapt those helpful insights and methods to my own setting without compromising sound theology or the ethical boundaries in which I was responsible to operate.

Likewise, ministers and future ministers working through this book must use appropriate lenses to apply the basic areas covered in this book to their particular context, ideally in conjunction with mentors, teachers, and colleagues.

These are the key areas addressed in this book:

- *The Minister as a Professional.* What kind of professional are we to be in a congregation that has certain expectations for their minister? How do the Bible and Christian theology inform our approach to this unique profession?

- *The Minister's Priorities.* The uniqueness of ministry requires the establishment of certain priorities concerning the relationships in the minister's life. We also need consistent tools to assist us in maintaining those proper, theologically sound priorities in all relationships.

- *The Minister's Communication.* How we communicate is as important as what we communicate, and we are responsible to create an environment where healthy communication, both publicly and privately, can flow.

- *The Minister and Conflict.* This specialized context for communication merits its own chapter since conflict is inevitable in all relationships and requires a special approach.

- *The Minister as Caregiver and Counselor.* Regardless of the extent of their training, ministers are often called upon to give godly counsel. Knowing healthy ethical boundaries can allow us both to help others and to engage other professionals in the community to facilitate spiritual and emotional maturity.

- *The Minister as Preacher and Worshipper.* Preaching and participation in the leadership of worship provide opportunities for ministers to assist the church in communicating the mission of God ethically.

- *The Minister and the Business of the Church.* How can we assist the church in distinguishing itself from worldly ways of doing business? How can we model sound business practices in a way that both enhances our standing in the community and equips businessmen and businesswomen in our congregations to be witnesses in the marketplace?

- *The Minister and Failure.* We all fail at times, and some even fall in regard to their calling, ordination vows, and relationships. How can we proceed after failure? How can we create an environment of redemption and grace when there has been a severe moral or ethical failure?

I hope this book becomes a tool for new pastors and those who mentor them, including students in Christian ministry and seminary programs, by giving voice to the practical areas of ethical importance that help define our calling as ministers of the gospel. For pastors who do not have mentors or even accountability partners, perhaps this book will provide motivation to intentionally seek such relationships in order to develop a fruitful, accountable, and Christ-centered ministry. At the end of each chapter, the mentoring questions and suggested readings assist readers in taking the concepts of this book to a deeper level as needed in their particular context.

Given the waning reputation of clergypersons over the past two decades, and with many denominations facing consequences related to poor ethical decision-making and poor preparation for such matters, may this book refocus our conversation about Christian ministry away from numbers, marketing, and politics, and toward our identity as Christians and Christian leaders who draw men and women of all ages to the mission of God in the world.

## ADDITIONAL TOOLS IN THIS BOOK

There are two appendices in this book. Appendix A contains a group of covenants that Christian leaders can share with their congregations to establish clear communication regarding ministerial boundaries. These covenants provide both a clear understanding of healthy boundaries for parishioners and healthy accountability for those of us who are leaders in Christian ministry. These agreements articulate a minister's desire for a healthy ethical environment.

Appendix B contains case studies that can be discussed among Christian leaders in a mentor relationship, in class-rooms, and among boards and staff members. The case studies address the kinds of real-life situations encountered in Christian ministry. Feel free to alter the questions or situations as needed. The studies are an amalgam of actual cases drawn from numerous sources and experiences, which is done to ensure the privacy of those represented.

The most technical portions of this book are found in chapter 1, which provides a brief introduction to the academic foundations of ethics in general and Christian ethics in par-ticular. Since the chapter contains materials that are often cov-ered in an entire semester of an ethics course, it moves quickly through several technical terms. This chapter establishes an important foundation, but I urge readers to take a closer look at the additional resources cited in the chapter to provide greater depth. All of the chapters of this book can be used separately as reference material that applies to specific ethical situations; however, the book does build upon the foundation of the first two chapters and uses them as lenses for setting ethical boundaries in the more specific areas of clergy life discussed in the ensuing chapters.

## PREVENTATIVE MAINTENANCE AND SPIRIT-LED HEALTH

Though this book does provide up-front measures that can prepare our churches and ourselves for a healthy, ethical environment for ministry, it can also be used as a tool to help reestablish healthy boundaries in areas long neglected. Also, the final chapter addresses ways to create an environment of confession, forgiveness, and restoration in situations where up-front maintenance did not occur or was ignored. Please note that all examples and case studies in this book are composites of the stories and experiences of a wide range of pastors with whom I have been acquainted and about whom I have read over the last two decades. Although many of these may sound familiar, no story in this book is a complete reproduction of any one story.

The sign in the mechanic's window represents sound theology. The Bible consistently reminds us to be prepared, to stay alert, and to remain ready. With a little preventative maintenance, our window sign could read: "I am paying now . . . so I am ready for whatever comes next!"

## Mentoring Questions

1. Discuss times when preventative maintenance helped you in a real-life situation.

2. List three areas where up-front communication and preparation would assist in your current ministry context.

3. Pray for God's direction as you enter into the mentoring process and make preparations for a long-term ministry.

## Suggested Reading

Daniels, T. Scott. *The First 100 Days: A Pastor's Guide.* Kansas City: Beacon Hill Press of Kansas City, 2011.

Meier, Paul, and Frank Minirth, et al. *What They Didn't Teach You in Seminary.* Nashville: Thomas Nelson, 1993.

Rowell, Jeren. *Thinking, Listening, and Being: Wesleyan Pastoral Disciplines.* Kansas City: Beacon Hill Press of Kansas City, 2014.

Willimon, William. *Pastor: The Theology and Practice of Ordained Ministry.* Nashville: Abingdon Press, 2002.

# THE ART OF MINISTRY ETHICS

1

Baseball player Ichiro Suzuki is an unlikely major league star. He is only five feet nine inches tall and weighs about 170 pounds. He is from Japan, and since 2003 the right fielder has become the most successful Japanese position player (non-pitcher) in Major League Baseball history. Suzuki discovered early on that he had baseball talent, but even in Japan, where people tend to be smaller in stature than those in the United States, there were concerns about his size. Ichiro spent most every day doing basic drills—hitting, fielding, and throwing—and keeping his body in the best shape possible. He added muscle to his small frame, which weighed only around 120 pounds when he got the opportunity to play professional baseball in Japan in his early twenties. Before long Ichiro got a contract in the majors, and the rest is history.

To this day, Ichiro, who is now over forty, wakes up twice a night to stretch. He is usually the first person on the field, stretching and warming up before the game, and he is known for doing a series of stretches before each pitch. He says that these disciplines not only keep him loose but also prepare him to make big plays when needed. He knows his body and mind will be ready when extraordinary opportunities arise. These practices have paid off because Ichiro has amassed nearly 3,000 career hits, a milestone few players have accomplished.

As a little league coach for several years, I found that young players often wanted to practice the big plays. Long before they had mastered the basics of the game, they would say, "Hit a pop-up that I have to chase to the wall" or "Throw me a pitch I can hit out of the park." Many kids even tried to adopt the unusual hitting style of Ichiro. Time and time again these young players would be disappointed that they were not able to produce the same results by simply copying Ichiro's mannerisms. "Put in the hours and years of stretching, practicing, and doing the basics that Ichiro has done, and then you can maybe try using his style," I would tell them. "Until then, try a basic stance!" In any sport, the best plays—those that show up on the television highlight reel—happen when players who are well trained in the basics of the game respond instinctively, based upon their years of preparation and experience. One does not start with the highlight plays.

Preventative maintenance is about preparing as much as you can up front while staying within the ethical boundaries of your calling as a disciple and minister of Christ. Through constant, ethical preparation, actions, and reflection, you will become more prepared to improvise when the opportunities arise.

Often I have been amazed at an athlete who makes an incredible play or a jazz musician who improvises a captivating solo. More than once I have heard players I have coached or fellow musicians ask, "How do they do that?" The answer is that they have prepared up front in basic ways that allow them to excel and even do the extraordinary when called upon. This is the idea behind preventative maintenance.

## MINISTRY JAZZ

Great jazz musicians such as Duke Ellington, Miles Davis, and Wynton Marsalis are known for their improvisational skills. At first glance, these musicians and others like them appear reckless or untrained. That is, until you hear them play a solo! Then something amazing takes shape. Yet those amazing "off the page" solos are not made up of random notes. Nor do they happen simply because the players abandon the written score. One need only to listen to a beginning jazz player to understand that bad improvisation is worse than badly played written notes! Every jazz player knows that it takes more than freedom to create good improvisation. That *something* is what I am calling preventative maintenance. In the case of the jazz musician, just as in the case of the athlete, the ability to improvise when called upon is the result of careful preparation in basic areas. The best jazz musicians, such as trumpeter Wynton Marsalis, are intricately acquainted with the basics of music: chord structure, key signatures, music theory, and even the limits of their instrument. From this springs the freedom to improvise in a way that contributes to the overall piece they are performing. Improvisation also is a way of stamping something of their own personality upon the song, but good improvisation is more about being true to the spirit and parameters of the song being performed by the whole group.

Ethicist Samuel Wells titles his introduction to the study of Christian ethics *Improvisation: The Drama of Christian Ethics.*[1] His central aim is to remind the church that the consistent practices of the church "shape and empower Christians" to become a "community of trust in order that it may faithfully encounter the unknown future without fear."[2] Likewise,

Marva Dawn and Eugene Peterson remind us that Christianity through the ages has "passed down the unfinished drama of God" and that like well-trained actors in an unfinished Shakespeare play, we "immerse ourselves" in the acts we do have so that we can adequately "improvise the parts that are missing."[3]

This is an ideal starting point for ethics in the context of Christian ministry. Preventative maintenance is not about preparing for every possible outcome or conflict. Rather, preventative maintenance assists us in creating healthy environments up front, using suggested boundaries and tools of reflection to prepare us in the best way possible for the unexpected. And ministry is definitely full of the unexpected! As Dawn and Peterson remind us, we immerse ourselves in the language of faith, sing the songs that draw us together in this faith, and "talk with the church throughout the ages as it expresses what it means to follow Jesus."[4] Furthermore, making adequate preparations and being intentional about creating a healthy ethical environment express our confidence in God's ability to work through us in the long run, not simply on the spur of the moment.

The preparation involved in becoming an ethical minister—that is, a minister whose personal and professional ethics reflect the ways and mission of Jesus Christ—suggests that there will be certain key principles that will inform our decisions regardless of the consequences we may experience. In other words, there will be "to die for" principles upon which we will stand no matter what. At other times, we will evaluate the goodness of our actions by evaluating the likely results of our actions. That includes times when we do our best to weigh the results of what could be two good choices. Weighing which of two or more good choices to make is usually the majority of the decision-making in which we engage in ministry. Some call this "ministering in the gray." At all times, we are called to be bathed in prayer, to consistently participate in worship and discipleship, and to evaluate our actions and decisions in light of the ways of God acted on our behalf through the love and grace of Jesus Christ. Stated in a more formal way, as will be explained briefly in the next section, our ethical decisions come from *deontological* approaches (up-front values that we hold regardless of consequences), *teleological* approaches (determinations based upon the overall result or goal of an action or decision), and approaches that are identified with *virtue ethics* (good actions and decisions produced by a transformed character through participation in the community of faith). What follows is a very brief overview of these key principles, which provide foundational paradigms for the study of and the participation in ethics.

## HOW WE MAKE ETHICAL DECISIONS

"What is right is right!" "Don't let our secular culture dictate our ethics!" "All's well that ends well!" These sayings remind us that there are varying ways to understand right and wrong. These phrases also remind us that a variety of factors influence how we decide what is good.

In the formal study of ethics, there are several categories of values, which are the things we hold dear individually and as a society. Developing a system of values—things considered good or right—begins with cultural *norms*. *Norms* are consistent modes of behavior that a culture adopts as acceptable over a period of time. In established communities, cultural norms become ways, for example, that a community recognizes who is "in" or who is a normal part of the community. In church life, a norm may express itself in something as small as seating arrangements in the worship service or the order of service itself. Over time, key norms become ingrained into the community and more universalized as acceptable. In these cases, the norms become *mores* or *values*.

Cultural *mores* are those consistent behaviors that the community deems as key to the community's identity. The set of beliefs that elevate norms (normative behaviors) to the level of *mores*, or "moral behaviors," are *values*. *Values* are deeply held beliefs of individuals and communities that become normative representations of what the individual or culture deems as good. These values become the basis for ethical systems, sometimes called *systems of morality*. Key aspects of these ethical systems become codified into *laws*. Every system runs the risk of elevating culturally specific norms to the level of universal values. This is why a consistent ethical system becomes the key to filtering out what is essential and what is a passing fad or simply preferred by a particular group.

For instance, the so-called Jim Crow laws, which enforced racial segregation in the United States, especially in the South, are examples of accepted norms that were codified into laws. However, these laws and mores explicitly excluded certain groups (especially African-Americans but also poor Caucasians at times). Although most of us today would rightly consider those mores and laws unjust and unfair, their power was so prevalent that, as one Southern historian observed, questioning them at the time was as difficult for most whites to do as it would have been for a fish to critique its water![5]

As members of the church of Jesus Christ, we, too, are immersed in a system—called a kingdom by Jesus—that has norms and mores. But these ways are not based in power, nor do they find their authority in ever-changing human opinions and comfort levels. We are called to operate from a system that shines light in a dark world and can face even the gray without fear.

*Ethics* is a systematic approach to assessing what is right or wrong, or what is good and bad. As H. Ray Dunning reminds, mores are what we learn to do, and ethics describes why we do what we do.[6] An ethical system measures right and wrong in regard to some *authority* (a term we will describe in more detail below) and in the context of a *community*. All of these elements are crucial to a full-fledged *ethical system*: a way of consistently measuring right and wrong based upon an accepted authority in the context of a particular community. Since this is a book about Christian clergy ethics, it is important now to examine those key elements of an ethical system in this particular context. We will consider each element of the ethical system below.

## Authority

In popular thought, authority is closely associated with power. Someone or something is an authority simply because he or she is in a position of power. While there are power-based approaches to authority, the technical definition of authority is as follows: that which someone *allows* to change his or her actions and/or attitudes. Note the key word *allows*. Real, lasting authority, according to the technical ethical definition, is granted.

Authority also results in consistent change in actions or attitudes or both. This is why authority granted upon position or power is limited: it does not produce long-term change in attitude or behavior.

Consider one of the most extreme forms of power-based authority, torture. The victim of torture may indeed consent to say or do something in response to the immediate power-based manipulation he or she experiences. However, studies show that this sort of manipulative control is short-lived and often inaccurate where information or change of behavior is concerned. When the one being overpowered is free from the torturer's grasp, he or she will most often resort back to previous ways of thinking or acting. This demonstrates the relative short-term influence of power-based authority.

Jesus came without power or prestige. For Jesus, the basis of authority—which, again, in ethics describes a consent-based change of actions or attitude—is love. The love of God expressed through Jesus has a compelling, not a coercive, effect. As Paul writes, "For Christ's love *compels* us" (2 Cor. 5:14, emphasis added). For the Christian, especially the Christian minister, authority is derived from love-based actions that are compelling rather than coercive.

For Christians, God and, more specifically, God's ways as revealed through the person and work of Jesus Christ, is the source of authority. We learn of the story of God's redemptive love culminating in the person and work of Christ through Scripture, which Christians consider a special or specific revelation from God through human authors. This means that we allow God's ways as expressed in the person and work of Jesus Christ to change our attitudes and actions in accordance with God's purposes as expressed in Scripture.

An unbeliever does not consider God or the ways of Jesus Christ as an authority in the technical sense. A casual Christian who more consistently allows other loyalties (besides loyalty to the ways of Jesus Christ) to change his or her behavior and attitudes does not acknowledge or accept the authority of God either. Likewise, a minister who is driven, motivated, and changed by something other than the love expressed in the person and work of Christ and the purposes of God revealed in Scripture does not accept God as his or her authoritative guide.

Jesus Christ is the Source of the value system we call Christian ethics. Scripture is the authoritative source of revealing God's redemptive work culminating in Jesus. The church, created by Jesus (Matt. 16:18-20), is the repository and interpreter of God's ways revealed in Christ through Scripture. So for Christian clergy there is a progression of authoritative voices that ultimately includes the following:

- *The scriptural and theological basis of one's calling.* This refers to how you know you are called into ministry, and the theological basis of that call. This calling begins with a relationship with God through Christ, who is revealed in Scripture.

- *The voice of the church in affirming that calling.* One's place in vocational ministry, like one's authority, is granted, and in the case of the minister, this place is granted by the people of God, the church, to which (as stated above) is given the authority through Christ to affirm the call of those who serve as its servant leaders.
- *Creedal and governing statements and offices.* A strong ministry leader will be a loyal follower of his or her hierarchical authorities. For those in a congregationally governed, autonomous system, this may be simply the unified voice of a local congregation. For others, it is a formalized hierarchical structure that includes district and regional overseers or bishops. Even the apostle Paul, a strong and very vocal leader, calls upon Christians under his pastoral authority to "follow my example, *as I follow the example of Christ*" (1 Cor. 11:1, emphasis added).

When these sources of authority are taken seriously, the minister is free to improvise when needed in the gray areas of ethical decision-making. Furthermore, gaining credibility as a leader is easier when others see that we, too, are willing to be accountable to authority and to be loyal to those who lead us as they follow Christ. With a clear understanding and affirmation of the sources of our authority as ministers, we are better able to lead with consistency and integrity. We are not called to follow any authority blindly. This means that we must have some sense of hierarchy, a priority list of authorities, grounded in the authority of Scripture and sound Christ-centered theology.

## Community

Ethics is never done in a vacuum. That is to say, all ethical decisions and behaviors take place in a particular context: a community. For the Christian, that community is the church. The church consists of those who have been called together as Christ's community; they are the people who join together to live out the "way" of Christ: "Once you were not a people, but now you are the people of God" (1 Pet. 2:10). The church becomes the context in which Christian ethics is consistently practiced, while also being a cumulative voice through the ages of an authoritative means of interpreting God's revelation through Christ. Therefore, being rooted in consistent theology means being in harmony with the wisdom handed down through the church over time. This provides ethical consistency in our approach to ministry.

While not all local churches or church leaders consistently work from a place of health and integrity, being rooted in a Christian community gives us a far better chance of developing a consistently ethical ministry. As far as possible, then, the wisdom of the church (both local and global), the faith statements of the denomination with which one is affiliated, and the leadership and accountability personnel under which one serves should be taken seriously. In those rare cases where temporal church authorities in a particular church or denominational setting seem to oppose what the church has historically accepted as clear teaching, the minister must state clearly his or her doctrinal opposition to the will of the temporal authorities in place and be willing to accept whatever consequences may come, even if it means leaving a particular congregation or denomination. Jeren Rowell writes that for John Wesley, ecclesial authorities and the authority of the community of faith were to be held in highest regard. Rowell also observes that "the only exceptions Wesley seemed to tolerate had to do with those rare instances where a particular body would require its pastor to do something which Scripture forbids or if one were being required to omit something that Scripture clearly commands."[7]

Ethics, especially Christian ethics, is lived out in community. For Christians, this community is the community of faith—the church. The church is vital in helping us choose God's authority—God's ways—consistently in our lives and ministries. In Christ we are charged with assisting one another in keeping the main thing the main thing. While there are a variety of polities, or governmental systems, in church life, the consensus of the people of God who serve together in the church should guide the theological, ethical, and practical aspects of ministry.[8]

## SYSTEMS OF MEASUREMENT

Consistency is a key concept in developing an ethical system. The consistency of Christian ethics is measured through the lens of the person and work of Jesus Christ. The question here is whether there is a consistent measuring tool for determining whether a decision or action is ethically sound. For Christians, that tool, or measure, is the love of God expressed in Jesus Christ. This is our ethical *system*, which is actually more than a system. This system is not a static set of principles but instead focuses on the goals of an action. H. Ray Dunning reminds us that Christian ethics is more teleological (from the Greek word *telos*, meaning goal or aim) than it is deontological (from the term *deon*, meaning duty, which describes a preestablished rule).[9]

There are three types of ethical systems. First, *deontological*, or duty-based, systems emphasize established principles that will not be altered regardless of the outcome of the ethical decision. Second, *teleological*, or goal-based, systems take seriously the outcome or consequences of an ethical decision in determining right and wrong. And finally, *virtue ethics* refers to systems that concentrate on the transformation of the individual into a person of integrity whose actions will therefore result in good.

No one system of ethics is completely isolated from the other two. However, if we are to evaluate our decisions and how they are made in order to be *consistent* in our ethic, we must understand these approaches in a bit more detail. The following is a very basic overview, so consulting an introductory ethics text is recommended for a more detailed analysis of these approaches to ethics.

## Three Types of Ethical Systems

### *Duty-Based Systems*

Some ethical decisions are made up front. In other words, some values are so dear to us that we will act in that particular way regardless of the outcome or consequences. An early mentor of mine once said, "Know what you are willing to die for, and know what is not worth dying for." If we have a true sense of calling, we likely have some "to die for" issues. After all, as Martin Luther King Jr. often said (as paraphrased here), "If we have nothing to die for, then we have nothing worth living for."[10] Of course, some of these issues may change over time. This is a healthy part of our growth as ministers of the gospel. As we mature, some methods or even theological positions we once held as essential will seem less important. Regardless, any time we take an ethical stand or approach that has little or no dependence upon consequences or outcomes, we are acting *deontologically*. This approach to ethics is based upon the thought of Immanuel Kant, the eighteenth-century philosopher who wrote: "Do everything you do as if it will become universal law."[11] This means that some aspects of ethical decision-making rely on the principle involved, regardless of what the outcome may be. Firefighters who rush toward a burning building even though everyone else is running away and know they may experience some harm, but they do this because it is their duty to do so. This is deontological ethics in a nutshell: doing one's duty for a higher purpose, regardless of the immediate consequences. In ministry, this may involve refusing to make certain changes in a particular theological position, even though changing the position would likely bring about immediate growth in church attendance.

Deontological approaches to ethics are also called non-consequentialist since the determination of right and wrong does not depend upon the consequences or results of the ethical choice made. This approach also is sometimes referred to as Kantian ethics due to Kant's influence upon this way of thinking. This approach reminds us that there are things worth dying for—worth doing because they are considered innately good regardless of the outcome. Weaknesses of deontological ethics include its inflexibility and its inability to assist us when two or more important principles or duties compete. At its worst, deontological ethics can become legalistic. Fortunately, there are other ways to measure ethical decisions.

### Goal-Centered Systems

Teleological ethics emphasizes the determination of good or right from the consequences of a choice. Since consequences or results matter greatly in this approach, it is often referred to as consequentialist ethics. In Christian ethics, teleological ethics measures the goodness of an act or of a decision based upon the way in which the act or decision amplifies the love of God. That which produces the most Christlike, loving result is good according to a teleological approach.[12] At its worst, teleological ethics can seem to allow the ends to justify the means. This means that the most extreme versions of consequentialist ethics may advocate virtually any approach or method of achieving a particular goal or end so long as the goal is achieved. Fortunately, this is not normally the way in which teleological ethics are employed, especially in Christian contexts.

At its best, a teleological approach can assist us in determining right or wrong when two duties or values seem to be in competition. For instance, I may believe that it is my duty to be a good citizen and obey the law. I may also believe that human life is valuable. If I were to walk past a pond posted with a "No Trespassing" sign and hear the voice of boy who had fallen into the pond and was drowning, I could no longer rely upon my sense of duty alone. I would choose to elevate the value of human life over the value of being a good citizen, which means I would ignore the sign, jump into the pond, and save the drowning boy. By doing so, I would be demonstrating a teleological, or consequentialist, approach to ethics. In church life, there are times when ministers and church leadership teams evaluate a decision based upon the outcome—that is, will this decision move us closer toward the goals of our mission, or should we attempt another approach, one that is also within the scope of our mission but possibly more effective?

Though we might think that deontological, or nonconsequentialist, ethics are the norm for the Bible, theologians including H. Ray Dunning argue that the Bible's approach is more teleological—that is, more goal-oriented or consequentialist.[13] This means that although there are many deontological aspects of Scripture (things that are considered right regardless of the consequences), the overarching goal of biblical ethics is to advance God's goals in the world (a teleological, or consequentialist, approach). Rahab the prostitute, who lied to protect the Canaanite spies from being discovered and killed, is called righteous for doing so (Josh. 2:4-6; Heb. 11:31). If we rely upon a strictly deontological view, we have a quandary in regard to Rahab's story: we value telling the truth, and we also value the lives of those who are fulfilling God's mission. Rahab's story is not a blanket excuse for lying. However, when two important duties or principles collide, we are called to take a further step and evaluate the situation teleologically. The question then becomes: How do we familiarize ourselves with the goals of God in the world so that our ethical decision-making furthers the promotion of those goals? The answer lies in the third key ethical category: virtue ethics.

### Virtue Ethics

Virtue ethics describes an approach to ethics that emphasizes the character development of an individual. In philosophical ethics, one becomes more virtuous by exposing oneself to and acting upon key virtues such as courage, compassion, bravery, or patience. In Christian ethics, one becomes more virtuous by being, in the words of Scripture, "transformed into [the Lord's] image with ever-increasing glory" (2 Cor. 3:18).

This means that participation in Christian devotion, corporate worship, and the mission of compassion all work together to transform us into people who embody and share the love of Jesus Christ. We are transformed by consistently interacting with the liturgy—the worship of God by God's people using the elements of worship handed down through Scripture, the early church, and liturgies through the centuries. These include prayer (the prayers of the church found in Scripture and key liturgies, along with extemporaneous prayers), Scripture, giving, music, preaching, and the Eucharist. During worship, these words and interactions shape us into what we are to exemplify throughout the week.

Sundays, not Mondays, set the tone and rhythm for Christians and therefore develop within us the virtues that make us representatives of Christ and of his mission in the world. We will explore the specific contributions of each of these elements of worship in a later chapter. But for now, we note that *Christian virtue ethics* refers to the way in which we are shaped by consistent exposure to the ways of God, the people of God, and worship of God.[14]

# ETHICAL DECISION-MAKING PRACTICES

## The Ethics Grid

Given the foundational issues we have discussed so far, we can begin to utilize an ethical grid through which to process the key considerations in making Christ-centered ethical decisions.[15] This grid comprises four quadrants, each representing a related key element in ethical decision-making, moving from highest to lowest in importance of authority.

### 1. The Theological Quadrant

The theological quadrant involves asking questions such as these: What theological considerations are important in addressing this situation? Is our approach to this decision distinctly Christian, or does it follow some nontheological pattern or norm? Is this decision in harmony with our understanding of the mission of Christ in the world, the mission of the church, and the vision and mission of our local church?

### 2. The Priorities Quadrant

The priorities quadrant leads us to consider these questions: Does this decision reveal our desire to maintain scriptural priorities in our congregation? Does this decision take into account the boundaries of our theology and the boundaries of the law? Will this point individuals and families toward Christ, or will it simply clutter their calendar with items that may actually be in competition with Christ-centered priorities? Are we making the good name of the church more of a priority than a convenient or inexpensive opportunity? Are there up-front principles that we will follow regardless of the outcome or popularity of this decision (deontological elements)? What assessments should we make to estimate the outcome of the decision (teleological elements)?

### 3. The Character Quadrant

The character quadrant requires questions such as these: Is this something we can share publicly without fear of casting a negative shadow on the character of Christ? Will this cast a negative shadow on any of the decision-makers and participants in the decision? Does this decision and the manner in which it is made project integrity to the church, to the community, and to the world (virtue ethics)?

### 4. The Relational Quadrant

This quadrant delves into questions such as the following: Is our approach to this decision fostering a healthy environment for strong, Christ-honoring relationships? Does this decision take seriously the mission of Christ to the congregation with which we have been entrusted? Does this decision take seriously Christ's desire for everyone—even the traditionally marginalized voices of our community—to have a voice? Does this decision rely on healthy methods of communication or avoid approaches to communication in a way that may lead to long-term harm to the community in order to achieve the non-Christlike goal of appeasement? Does this decision pay due regard to established authorities in our local church and denomination?

A sample grid that can serve as a reproducible work sheet for decision-making is found in Appendix A.

## The Usefulness of the Grid

All of these aspects should be considered when making an ethical decision in church life. Otherwise, it becomes tempting for churches to act pragmatically, basing whether a decision is good or right simply upon what is practical for the moment. Overuse of pragmatic approaches can cause well-meaning ministers and churches to gradually stray from their identity as theologically based communities of faith that pattern themselves after the ways of Jesus Christ. They become like a ship whose captain forsakes the use of the compass in favor of personal intuition and eventually strays miles away from the intended course. Asking key ethical questions based upon our Christian identity keeps our ministry on course.

The Grid for Ethical Decision-Making (see Appendix A) is not a simple plug-and-play solution, but it does broaden the discussion for ministers and leadership teams faced with day-to-day decisions, most all of which have ethical implications. When we are intentional in submitting theological and ethical decisions through this kind of discussion grid, we practice preventative maintenance by shaping an ethical environment that maintains the theological focus of the church we are called to serve. Use of this grid does not prevent conflict; indeed, it may very well lead to conflict. However, that conflict will result from transparency, honest disagreement, and addressing possible ethical red flags, and it will contribute to the long-term health of the organization.

## Practices that Transform the Mind

Counselors are fond of saying that we learn to act ethically in two ways: Either we feel our way into action, or we act our way into feeling. If so, then sometimes our ethical actions flow from our internal values or feelings. At other times, we practice ethical actions and only later internalize them into virtues. The Bible and the history of Christian worship acknowledge the value of *both* approaches. In fact, Christian virtue ethics, as briefly introduced above, relies upon both approaches. This is why, in the context of Christian worship, we see repetition: repetition in our songs, prayers, Bible passages, and sacraments. Those of us who pray the Lord's Prayer each week would likely admit that there are weeks that these words are recited by rote. But because everyone else—the church body—is reciting it together, we say it as well. Over time, most of us have experienced moments when those words were far more than a mere recitation. In fact, the repetition of those words over a period of time can produce a change in our attitude, in our ways of thinking, and in our ways of acting.

This is similar to Paul's description of transformation as "the renewing of your mind" (Rom. 12:2). The word *mind* (*nous* in the Greek) here refers to our mind-set or way of thinking. Changing *how* we think and *what* we think influences how we act. Exposing ourselves consistently to Scripture, which teaches love for our enemies, for example, eventually influences our approach toward our enemies and our practice of forgiveness in general—sometimes even before our feelings catch up to our actions. We do not always feel like loving our enemies. However, we learn to do so by repeating Scripture, songs, and actions that remind us that God, through Jesus Christ, loves God's enemies, who once included us![16]

## THE TRUE NATURE OF OUR CALLING

The use of theologically grounded practices that take seriously the fact that, as ministers, we lead a *theological* organization creates a basis for actions in our transformed way of thinking: virtues that exalt the ethics of Christ. As Eugene Peterson reminds us, ministers today struggle to find their true identity and often wrestle with a variety of societally imposed roles: marketer, counselor, politician, human resources director, and administrator, just to name a few.[17] Certainly, aspects of these roles intersect with the oversight and care that pastors seek to give as part of their calling. However, as Peterson and others remind, it has become easy for pastors to forsake the scriptural and theological basis of their calling and substitute the duties and values of these other industries for the work of ministry.[18] This is where ethical dangers arise: ministers are not simply businesspeople who apply the values and models of the marketplace to the church. We are not elected officials who seek to motivate constituents through the language and tactics of politics in order to achieve God's mission in the world. We are not simply counselors, whose approach to ministry is primarily therapeutic. Certainly all of these professions intersect with what ministers do and inform us to some degree. However, we speak a different language: the language of Scripture, tradition, and theology. We share different values: the values espoused and lived out by Jesus Christ and those whom he calls the church. We strive for different goals: our measure of success is rooted in Christlike love and humility, and not secular models of success grounded in consumerism and power.

Only when we take seriously the theological grounding of our calling to minister will we serve in a manner consistent with the ethics of Jesus Christ and his kingdom. The following chapters cast a vision for ministry and the key roles of the minister that function in harmony with this theological identity: measuring success based upon God's ways, even when the world's measurements differ; seeking outcomes that further the kingdom of God and God's ways, even when they are unpopular; and always seeking to be transformed individually and as the community of faith into the image of Christ.

## Mentoring Questions

1. Can you think of occasions when you have seen ministry decisions made based upon simple pragmatism instead of theologically grounded approaches? Describe them.

2. Think of a key decision you have observed or have been part of making in church life and discuss it using the Ethics Grid described in this chapter. What would this grid have added to the discussion? How would it have altered the decision you are discussing?

## Suggested Reading

Dunning, H. Ray. *Reflecting the Divine Image: Christian Ethics in Wesleyan Perspective.* Eugene, OR: Wipf and Stock, 2003.

Grenz, Stanley J. *The Moral Quest: Foundations of Christian Ethics.* Downers Grove, IL: InterVarsity Press, 2000.

Trull, Joe, and James E. Carter. *Ministerial Ethics: Moral Formation for Church Leaders.* Grand Rapid: Baker Academic, 2004.

Wilkens, Steve. *Beyond Bumper Sticker Ethics: An Introduction to Theories of Right and Wrong.* Downers Grove, IL: InterVarsity Press, 2011.

## 2

# THE MINISTER AS A

# PROFESSIONAL

"We want a pastor, not a 'professional' clergyperson." So said a member of the interviewing committee to the young pastoral candidate in her first interview. Knowing the church's recent history of conflict, the young minister took the committee member's words as a cry for personalized ministry that would be available to hurting congregants and promote health and a clear vision for the future. The statement also reminded the ministerial candidate of a conflict she was having within herself about her sense of calling and her choice of professions, if indeed the pastorate was a profession at all. Is pastoral ministry a profession? Are pastors in the same category as doctors, lawyers, and even athletes who are all called "professionals"?

These questions, and the struggle experienced by this young minister, are common in Christian ministry. Most denominations require systematic preparation through education and supervised service, often for several years, before granting ordination. Many who sense a calling to Christian ministry receive undergraduate, graduate, and even postgraduate preparation, accumulating as many years of schooling as do lawyers, doctors, or scientists. All three of those fields are labeled as professions, and those who serve are expected to conduct themselves "professionally." This means that they are expected to acquire a consistent course of training, seek continuing education throughout their careers, and conduct themselves in a manner consistent with ethical standards in their fields.

Pastors are expected to have similar characteristics. In this sense, then, members of the clergy are professionals. However, as noted in our introduction, the term *professional* as applied to a minister can have the connotation of one who is cold, aloof, and even disinterested in the very people being served. With this apparent dichotomy, it seems that the proper question for ministers is not are we professionals but rather what *kind* of professionals should we be?

## A DIFFERENT KIND OF PROFESSIONAL

The idea of the professional as cold and uncaring is certainly a hindrance in defining the role of a clergyperson as a professional one. However, the practitioner of any profession who viewed his or her status as a place from which to exercise cold, calculating control without a personal connection to clients would also be at a disadvantage. For example, the physician who consistently confuses patients with big words or presumes to make decisions without regard for their wishes would quickly be replaced if the patients had a choice in the matter—and they often do. Most prefer a physician who is both knowledgeable of the key concepts of medicine and able to convey these concepts in ways that provide caring and connection to the patient. Given the generally accepted standards of the medical profession, the physician who not only knows medicine but also demonstrates connection and caring to patients is the more professional. The stereotypically "professional" physician who is cold, uncaring, and paternalistic is not a true professional at all.

Why, then, can't those who make their living in Christian ministry be a healthy kind of professional? To do so would certainly require consistent training and continuing education, and it will also require a set of up-front ethical boundaries that assist in navigating the sometimes rough waters of ministering to others in the name of Christ. As pastoral theologian Gaylord Noyce reminds, "By announcing availability as a professional—'attorney at law,' 'M.D.,' 'pastor'—promises are made to the public."[1] Understanding and communicating these promises up front is the first step toward setting healthy ethical boundaries in pastoral ministry.

## THE PROMISES WE MAKE

When we enter the pastor's study and prepare for our week of ministry, what promises are we making as professionals, in the highest sense of the word? To answer this question, we begin by examining a key biblical model for the identity of a Christian minister and contrasting it with popular models that have emerged over the centuries. The expectations of others and even our own expectations of what we are to do can distract us from our essential calling. Therefore, it is essential to understand the biblical foundations of our work.

Like most ordained ministers, I have an ordination certificate on my wall. It includes a description of what I am expected and commissioned to do as an ordained minister of the gospel; included are phrases such as "a proper person to administer the sacraments," "feed the flock of God," and "hold fast to the form of sound words according to the established doctrines of the gospel." These phrases are truncated versions of the words uttered by the overseers who placed their hands on my head as I knelt with my wife over twenty years ago. These words were more directly taken from Scripture: "Preach the word; be prepared in season and out of season; correct, rebuke and encourage—with great patience and careful instruction" (2 Tim. 4:2). Within this verse are found key biblical foundations for the office of "elder" or "overseer" or "pastor." Ministers are to proclaim the message of Christ and his ways (preach), give wise counsel and correction, faithfully exemplify the character of Christ, remain doctrinally sound, and render care that will point others to Christ. In addition, ministers are called to administer the sacraments of the church. These key biblical elements of the call to ministry are always in a sort of "competition" with other professional models that, while helpful and instructive in some areas, stray from the consistent biblical model to which the minister is called.

Retired Methodist bishop William H. Willimon provides a helpful list of what ministry is *not*, based upon stereotypical models of ministry. Willimon's list of contemporary images of the professional pastor include media mogul, political negotiator, therapist, manager, activist, preacher, and servant.[2] There may be elements of overlap with each of these concepts, but these images do not clearly define the work of the pastor as professional. Given the prevalence and power of these competing models, it is easy for the essential biblical and theological elements of pastoral identity to be subsumed to popular versions of our role. Indeed, Willimon suggests that "contemporary ministry is groping for an appropriate metaphor for our pastoral work."[3]

The late ethicist William F. May provides a summary list of positive roles of the minister based upon a biblical model. May's list of terms that follow a biblical, historical, and theologically sound definition of the role of the minister are foreign to our culture and will require not only up-front statements of preventative maintenance but also consistent revisiting and education. May's list includes: *priest* (the role of the minister in regard to baptism, liturgy, and prayer), *prophet* (the minister as teacher and illuminator of God's presence in the world), *servant* (ministering to the needs of the congregation and to those outside the church in order to connect them with the kingdom of God), and *leader* (though May notes that the kind of leadership ministers provide is, to use Niebuhr's expression, as "priest of priests, teacher of teachers, and a counselor of counselors"[4]).

As we create up-front boundaries that shape our pastoral calling and work, we make use of biblical and theological considerations to redefine the terms associated with professional ministry. This has a twofold effect. First, it keeps the minister from burnout and from other personal and professional blunders associated with performing tasks outside his or her calling. Good up-front boundaries help us discern what we should and should not spend time on in day-to-day ministry. Second, creating these boundaries sets the congregation at ease regarding what the pastor does all week and invites parishioners to assist in the overall vision of ministry. If the perception of the minister's professional promise is that he or she "does all of the evangelism and teaching," then those with gifts of evangelism and teaching may not feel that they have a place. If pastoral care is perceived to be the responsibility of the pastor only, then aspects of care will be missed, even in smaller congregations. If, however, the minister leads as one who is serving, equipping, teaching, and helping to form others while he or she is also being formed in the community of Christ, then ministry fulfills the call of Christ to be the church in the world.

Our professional promise to a congregation, based upon the brief discussion of ordination above and the biblically distinctive role of the minister and community, may go something like this:

> As one called and trained for ministry, I will do my best to take initiative in the Christ-centered oversight of our vision, I will take seriously my role as one who prays and who preaches and teaches Scripture, I will be consistently present in the lives of those in our congregation and community, especially the ill and poor, and I will assist others in discovering ways in which they can grow in their faith and gifting through empowered service in Christian ministry.

This professional covenant can be altered to fit the role of an individual minister or Christian leader, of course. It is an example of the kind of clear, up-front promise that sets biblical boundaries regarding the minister's call. It is a statement that says, "I am a trained professional who takes my calling from God seriously," while at the same time declaring that the minister is a particular kind of professional, one who values the role more than the title, and who will use his or her gifts and training to facilitate the inclusion of others into the kingdom of God.

## A TRINITARIAN MODEL OF PROFESSIONALISM

The Trinitarian God described in orthodox Christian theology is loving and communal by very nature. This God, who *is* perfect community, seeks to create this same kind of loving community among people: a community that is distinct (Gen. 1:26-27) yet indivisible (in harmony with God and with each other). Three practical implications of the triune nature of God help us understand the kind of people God desires us to be. These key traits help define what kind of professionals we ministers are called to be.

First, the Trinity teaches us humility. The relationships within the Trinity are not hierarchical, with the Father somehow outranking the Son and the Spirit. Rather, there is mutuality. Within that mutuality, we see humility. This is seen most clearly in Jesus's self-emptying, emphasized in Philippians 2 and exemplified in Jesus's prayers to the Father (see Matt. 11:25-26) and in Jesus's surrender of his will to that of the Father (Luke 22:42), even though Jesus and the Father "are one" (John 10:30). For the minister, the Trinitarian ethic of humility produces a professionalism defined by respect for those to whom we minister. If the Son of God, who was God "in very nature" (see Phil. 2:6), demonstrated humility and mutuality toward others, then we, too, must demonstrate this in our profession of ministry. Mutuality means that we do not "lord it over" those around us (Matt. 20:25) but seek harmony, consensus, and participation in the work of the ministry. This biblical and Trinitarian understanding of professionalism is much different from one based primarily on skills, training, or charisma—the traits often associated with secular versions of professionalism.

Second, the Trinity teaches us the importance of community. The Trinity shows us God's desire to reproduce community.[5] God, who by very nature *is* community, seeks to reproduce that same kind of loving and harmonious community. For clergy, working outside of or above the community in which we are placed—either as unapproachable hermits or heavy-handed rulers in our congregations—is contrary to the Trinitarian model God himself desires to reproduce in the community God has created, the church.[6]

Third, the Trinity teaches us the importance of engaging in persuasion over coercion or manipulation. The communication Jesus modeled for us is based on invitation: wooing rather than forcing. Ministers who abuse their positions to manipulate others instead of lovingly persuading them work in contrast to the Trinitarian model of professionalism. There is no trickery or strong-arming within the Trinity, and leaders in the community God seeks to reproduce will shun deceptive or bullying models of professionalism. Persuasion does not imply slick salesmanship. The integrity modeled by the members of the Trinity in their mutual interaction is what distinguishes the professionalism of the clergy from that of some secular counterparts. Interestingly, many business leaders are discovering that this model of professionalism (though not explicitly denoted as Trinitarian) is the most effective approach to developing strong and lasting relationships within their companies and with their customers.

Like conductors in an orchestra, ministers facilitate harmony. Harmony is an important theological and relational concept, especially among cultures that place a high value on the concept of community. In much of African theology, for instance, the concept of harmony parallels the musical idea: many voices but in the same key. Each harmonious voice has a distinctive note but assists the others in creating the song. So too in a Christian community; though we are different, we help each other sing in the same key—the ways of Jesus Christ.[7] The key takeaway concerning the profession of ministry that we gain from the mystery of the Trinity is this: the God who is harmonious community calls his ministers to facilitate harmonious community among the people of God. There is always room in the choir for more!

## ONGOING CLARIFICATION

When any boundaries are set in life or in ministry, there will be those who push against them. Just as people had a wide variety of ideas regarding what kind of Messiah Jesus should be (see John 6–8), there is a wide variety of ideas regarding the professional role of the clergyperson. This is true even if the term *professional* is not used. One aspect of preventative maintenance for ministers is preparing to clarify and even correct false notions of our calling. How do we do this? It is critical to have an up-front and clearly communicated description of our calling and gifts. That description should be biblically based, send a clear message of service rather than of power, and have specific boundaries that clarify what ministry is and is not.

These statements are usually best prepared in collaboration with trusted mentors, denominational guides, and even other leaders within the congregation or place of service. The dialogue generated around the creation of a professional statement, which is best titled a "Theological Statement of Christian Ministry," will become a touchstone for preventative maintenance. Furthermore, having engaged in dialogue to create the statement, the minister can remind those who push the boundaries of the statement or even reject it outright that the statement was not formed in a vacuum. Rather, it is a biblically based and community-based statement that, while not perfect, is a tool for clear communication and understanding.

## WHAT COMES NEXT

Having clarified the type of professional minister you intend to be by forming a clear theological statement of ministry, and having established general boundaries for your ministerial role, you can explore other areas of preventative maintenance in more specific realms of ministerial service. Relationships are based upon agreements, and having an up-front agreement on what a minister does and how success in that job is to be measured will assist those whom we serve to join us in carrying out the ministry of Jesus Christ in the community and in the world.

Furthermore, as I have often said to ministerial candidates, we have to be able to look ourselves in the mirror at the end of the day and know that we have functioned with integrity. Clarifying the biblical basis for who we are and what we do gives us that sense of peace and satisfaction, especially when ministerial success is difficult to measure on paper. When we have clarity on the theological and ethical bases of our calling, we are able both to clearly communicate the uniqueness of our role as Christian ministers and to provide a tool for accountability that adequately reflects our participation in the mission of God in the world. While we will often learn from professions outside our own, having this clear statement of our role helps to ensure that we benefit from the example of other professions without compromising the essential theological basis of our own calling.

## Mentoring Questions

1. What can you do to make *professional* a more positive word in association with the role of clergy?

2. Describe how a clergyperson might develop a professional demeanor without being cold or aloof.

3. Name specific ministry opportunities in which congregations expect what they think of as a more "professional" approach, that is, involving a higher degree of training and dedication.

## Suggested Reading

Jones, Gregory L., and Kevin R. Armstrong. *Resurrecting Excellence: Shaping Faithful Christian Ministry.* Grand Rapids: Eerdmans, 2006.

Noyce, Gaylord. *Pastoral Ethics.* Nashville: Abingdon, 1988.

Wind, J. P., et al. *Clergy Ethics in a Changing Society.* Louisville, KY: Westminster John Knox Press, 1991.

# 3

# CRITICAL RELATIONSHIPS

# IN MINISTRY

A young pastor, who was just a few years younger than I at the time, sat in my office and confessed that he was in an unhealthy relationship—with his church! He was, in his words, having an affair, not with a woman in the church but with the work of the ministry. This "holy mistress" was robbing him of time with his wife and children and destroying his marriage.

Because of the time and energy required to meet the many demands of Christian ministry, it is easy to become consumed by the work of the church. Ministry is honorable work, but it is the kind of work that, according to Scripture, requires a great deal of personal character and the establishment of priorities from ministers. There are few other jobs in which one's personal life, relationships, and priorities directly affect one's job description. Therefore, the minister must consistently evaluate these relationships and priorities and practice strong preventative maintenance in order to serve with integrity.

Developing healthy relationships is an important key to healthy Christian ministry. Most men and women enter ministry recognizing that, regardless of whether they are introverts or extroverts, dealing with people is an essential part of their calling. Introverts—those who are generally drained by people contact—have a tendency to bond with a few while keeping at a distance or even ignoring others in the congregation. Extroverts—those who tend to be energized by interaction with people—may spread themselves too thin among the congregants, leaving them to speculate about the depth of the care the extroverted pastor provides. The good news is that both extroverts and introverts can have fruitful ministries. Recognizing personal tendencies and compensating for areas of weakness or vulnerability can help you become comfortable with your own calling and unique personality.

Regardless of one's disposition, diving headfirst into pastoral ministry without establishing proper boundaries in relationships is a recipe for disaster. In particular, six key relationships must be kept in proper perspective to prevent a fruitful ministry from becoming a disaster. These relationships are, in order, with God, self, family, mentors and friends, parishioners, and the community. Together the six make up the essence of Christian ministry. They must be nurtured in specific ways to enable the minister to function effectively over a long period of time.

## RELATIONSHIP ONE: GOD

In her book *Leaving Church*, Episcopal priest and religion professor Barbara Brown Taylor speaks of a time early in her pastoral ministry in an Episcopal church in rural Georgia when she began to see cracks in her relationship with God and with the church. The demands of church life, which she loved at first and consistently met, began to take their toll on her most important relationship. She writes:

The demands of parish ministry routinely cut me off from the resources that enabled me to do parish ministry. I knew where God's fire was burning, but I could not get to it. I knew how to pray, how to bank the coals and call the Spirit, but by the time I got home each night it was all I could do to pay the bills and go to bed. I pecked God on the cheek the same way I did Ed [her husband], drying up inside for want of making love.[1]

For most who read these words, there will be an immediate and deep sense of empathy with Taylor and her feelings during this period in her ministry. Working for God often becomes a replacement for allowing God to work in and through us. Our relationship with God can become a means to an end instead of an end in itself, to paraphrase philosopher Immanuel Kant. We can easily make God a tool, a presence, or even a distant observer. Recapturing a sense of the presence of God in our hearts and in our daily calendars is both an ethical priority and a theological necessity. Otherwise, we may easily trade ethical Christian priorities in ministry for lesser ideals. As Greg Jones and Kevin Armstrong remind, "Christian life sets us on a journey of learning to have eyes to see and ears to hear God's work in the world. We need attentiveness to prayer, Scripture, Christian doctrine, and spiritual direction that can orient us toward friendship with God and cultivate right beliefs that will shape our practical reasoning."[2]

## RELATIONSHIP TWO: SELF

Like many in our mobile society, I have sat through more than my share of safety speeches by flight attendants. At such times, I am often distracted or impatient, but lately I confess that I have been interested in the portion of the safety speech regarding oxygen: "If you are sitting near someone who requires assistance with their oxygen mask, please adjust *your own mask first*, and then you will be able to assist others" (emphasis added). As I hear those words, I always think, *That is contrary to the natural inclinations of many of us.* Often when traveling I am seated near or beside one of my sons or my wife. Honestly, if an event occurred on an airplane in which I felt that oxygen deprivation was a problem, my first thought as a husband and a parent would be to move toward my loved ones and help them adjust their mask so that oxygen flowed properly before adjusting my own. As flawed and self-centered as we are, I predict that most people on the plane would have the same first thought, especially if a small child or a disabled loved one were nearby. This inclination is exactly why all airline safety speeches add this reminder. The thinking behind the reminder, according to one flight attendant I spoke with, is that your attempt at helping would be meaningless if you were passed out on the floor due to lack of oxygen. The result would be two casualties for the flight crew to handle rather than one.

To put it in a ministry context, in the words of one of my seminary professors: "Take care of yourselves, because the Lord can't use a dead saint like he can a live one!" It is very easy for ministers to overlook their own health precisely because their work is helping others. As in the case of low oxygen on an airplane, our initial reaction is to ignore our own needs so that we can care for others. There is a sense in which we are to, as the Bible reminds, look not only to our "own interests but . . . to the interests of the others" (Phil. 2:4). Ministry is not to be self-centered. However, the notion of "burning out for Jesus," as some have expressed it, is likely the result of poor self-care, which severely limits our ability to care for others in a long-term and consistent way.

If you and I as ministers are going to be in the proper frame of mind, heart, and health to minister to those on our priority list, we must be healthy ourselves. I attended one of the largest seminaries in America. Its library, classrooms, and other resources were quite impressive, as was the scope of the faculty. One surprising item on the campus of this seminary was a world-class gymnasium, complete with an aquatic center, cardiovascular facilities, free weights, and adjacent lighted tennis courts. I had attended a university with excellent workout facilities, but that seemed reasonable given the fact that the school was home to a Division I athletic program. The gym at this seminary would have been the envy of many Division I athletic programs. Intrigued, I asked a longtime professor about the gym. "The donors and trustees of the school who planned this facility included some of the leading doctors in the area," he told me. "They said they were tired of performing the heart surgeries and attending the funerals of so many out-of-shape pastors." The purpose of the gym was to increase the longevity and spiritual influence of the pastors trained there by helping them live longer and healthier lives. The trustees of the seminary saw prolonging the active lives of clergypersons by providing the means of healthy exercise as part of the overall mission of the school. Paul wrote, "For physical training is of some value, but godliness has value for all things, holding promise for both the present life and the life to come" (1 Tim. 4:8).

According to an article in *Leadership Journal*, many clergy tend to see self-care as selfish. Although pastors consistently suffer from hypertension, depression, and weight problems, relatively few take the time or energy required to adjust their lifestyles for better health. The article, which cites both researchers and pastors, notes that one solution to this trend involves reframing the conversation toward stewardship: in this case, stewardship of our own bodies. Just as pastors tend to be cautious about participation in activities that would be deemed unethical or immoral in order to guard their reputations, they can also steer themselves toward healthier lifestyle choices as a matter of witness. One denomination has renamed its emphasis on self-care as "stewardship of the body."[3]

Although not all seminaries can have state-of-the-art exercise facilities, all ministers can find consistent opportunities to care for their physical and spiritual well-being so they may be examples to God's flock and may provide consistent care for the people of God. Intensely busy schedules, stress, lack of consistent exercise, and improper diet all contribute to the ongoing health issues of pastors. Ethically, this affects ministers in at least two ways: longevity and witness. Self-care is a key starting point for being effective in the long run and to being effective and holistic in witness.

## RELATIONSHIP THREE: FAMILY

The most common casualty in Christian ministry is the minister's family. Clergy spouses and children are often on display and under pressure, and they seldom receive the accolades and praise—or the job satisfaction—of the clergyperson in the family. This does not mean that family members are not a vital part of any clergyperson's ministry. In fact, most ministers could not function without the prayers, work, support, and encouragement of their households. Unfortunately, the always-on-call nature of ministry is often a distraction for the minister even when he or she is physically present with family members. Pressures from parishioners, the community, and even ministerial overseers can push the clergyperson further and further into the demands of work and further away, emotionally and physically, from family.

For nearly two decades, I have served on ministerial boards in my denomination and have observed both good and bad examples of making family a high priority in ministry. When ministers pay proper attention to the needs of family, and when family members are made to feel more important than any other relationship except for the minister's relationship with God, the family tends to thrive and see the minister's calling as part of their own calling. This does not mean that the frequent relocations many ministers make do not bring difficult circumstances. However, clergy families who place a high priority upon consistent prayer, family care, and interaction tend to weather such storms and come out of them with an overall positive view of ministry and of life. Conversely, ministerial families in which the clergyperson consistently places church priorities ahead of family matters tend to experience long-term and often bitter resentment toward ministry.

Of course, some aspects of family time and relationships will suffer occasionally, as is the case for most professions. However, the difference between healthy and unhealthy relationships between a clergyperson and his or her family is consistency. It would be unrealistic to assume that any family could exist without occasional struggle or conflict, especially clergy families. Consistent evaluation of one's relationship priorities is a form of preventative maintenance in that it helps guard family time and relationships.

Practically speaking, this means that clergypersons should avoid the temptation to pattern their work lives after the shockingly workaholic lives of their nonclergy counterparts. Eugene Peterson, in his book *The Contemplative Pastor*, reminds clergy that it is not busyness that makes for a successful clergyperson. Indeed, busyness, according to Eugene Peterson, is often a sign of a lazy person or even an incompetent pastor, one who refuses to plan and prioritize.[4] While we may receive applause, even from ministry peers and overseers, for "burning ourselves out for God," the truth is that being an overworked clergyperson is a negative example to members of our congregation who are seeking an alternative to the loss of spiritual vitality and deep family connections that often accompany successful careers. To avoid falling into that trap, pastors must consistently evaluate the status of these important priorities—God and family. Here are a few helpful ways to keep these relationships in line.

## Be Intentional

It is ethically incumbent upon those of us in ministry to be consistently present *on purpose*. This is one of the struggles I have faced in the spiritual leadership of my own family. Early in my marriage, I often waited for my wife to initiate spiritual conversations or special times together. She was faithful to do this, but there were also times when she waited for me to take the initiative. In our conversations about this, I was reminded that I was often the initiator of spiritual matters and of special events in congregational life. Why should my family not receive the same intentional attention? Of course, ministry-related travel and certain congregational and denominational events continue to pose a challenge to me in consistently taking the initiative, and my wife has been faithful where I have fallen short. Yet she and my two sons have acknowledged their appreciation to me for intentionally scheduling times of spiritual enrichment along with fun times of interaction for our family. The consistency of the effort, even when my attempts are interrupted or fall short of the goals I have set, goes a long way in demonstrating that the spiritual well-being of my family members is even more important to me than the well-being of those whom I am called to pastor.

## Take Inventory

For married clergy, spouses are often the best gauge of our priorities. However, some others can share valuable reminders when our priorities go awry. Often, church leaders can be counted on to prompt us when they think we are not getting our church responsibilities done. We can also cultivate relationships with people who will ask about our time with God and our time with family. Jesus apparently trusted some people at a deep level. This inner circle of people, despite their flaws, was a deep source of comfort throughout his ministry. We will address mentorship below, a tool that provides

CRITICAL RELATIONSHIPS IN MINISTRY

yet another voice in the ongoing journey toward keeping our priorities in proper place.

## Guard Boundaries

I confess that saying yes to invitations to participate in additional ministries is exciting and often fulfilling for me. This is especially true when the invitation is an acknowledgment of particular gifts that I enjoy sharing with others, such as invitations to speak at a chapel service, to give a lecture, to present a paper, or to teach a course. All of these potential yeses are additional opportunities to minister in ways God has gifted me. But they are also potential opportunities to squeeze time with my family out of the picture, or even to affect aspects of my primary job, which is to minister to the congregation and community to which I am called. The best response to such invitations is not always no, but rather it is to say no when saying yes would break a promise in familial or congregational relationships. Furthermore, when yeses pile up to the point that they endanger personal spiritual growth, quality family time, or congregational trust, then no should become the default answer.

## RELATIONSHIP FOUR: MENTORS AND FRIENDS

In the novel *Gutenberg's Apprentice*, set in the late 1400s and tracing the development of Gutenberg's printing press, the narrator of the story—an apprentice to Gutenberg, the innovator of new printing methods that culminated in his history-changing printing press—reflects upon his early days as an apprentice in the art of copying. Copying by hand was the only means of mass-producing documents until the development of this new technology, the printing press. The apprentice reflects:

The work of the apprentice is the taming of all impulse: in place of pride, humility; impatience mastered, then subdued. It took Peter back to his first weeks at the scriptorium, where Anselm [his teacher] started by removing feathers, vellum, leather pouches, ornaments of every kind. He stripped the pupils down to one thin reed, a lump of lampblack, and one plain sheet. To learn the silencing of will, of the murky self: to strip their bodies and their minds to the essential. Apprenticeship, he said, was patience, and a deep, abiding faith: again, again, and yet again, until the hand was firm, the soul scoured clean. For only then would they be purely Adam's flesh, a conduit, a channel.[5]

Through the years of becoming prepared for ministry and of helping prepare others, I have found that mentoring relationships are crucial. To consistently maintain such relationships, I have had to proactively seek out mentors and mentees. Perhaps this book could become a tool in the creation of those relationships on a wider scale. Often, when there is a mutual desire for mentoring, the interactions are more reactive than proactive. This involves intense times of walking through crises together as they arise. This is important, of course. But, what if the relationship could also focus on preventative measures, "as iron sharpens iron," as Scripture reminds (Prov. 27:17)? What if proactive discussions about establishing healthy ethical boundaries up front were the focus of preparation for ministry, not only between a younger minister and his or her mentor but also among those who serve under the pastor's leadership? Again, the ultimate goal for this book is to provide resources for a healthy ministry that go hand in hand with healthy mentoring and accountability. Ministry throughout the Old and New Testaments was often done at least in pairs (for instance, Moses and Aaron in the Exodus account). Jesus and the early church leaders were known for sending out ministry teams "two by two" (Mark 6:7).

Throughout the Bible we see that men and women who kept their personal priorities in place and more effectively served in ministry had mentoring relationships. The patriarchs, the prophets, and the apostles all modeled mentoring relationships. Ministry is as much caught as it is taught, and mentoring relationships are key sources of encouragement, accountability, and lived-out instruction for Christian ministry. This is the biblical norm for preparation. Mentors assist us with blind spots in our approach to ministry by giving us an honest perspective on how we are carrying out the mission and on our vision of ministry. They help us check our motives and our methods in order to help us keep our priorities in proper perspective.

## RELATIONSHIP FIVE: PARISHIONERS

We still have a job to do, and the people of our congregation comprise our work environment. Like other professionals, we may use various tools; but, ultimately, these are put in place to, in the words of many ordination rituals, "shepherd the flock of God." The phrase itself appears in 1 Peter: "Be shepherds of God's flock that is under your care" (5:2). Peter's instructions on properly shepherding God's flock, paired with Paul's instructions to a young pastor named Timothy (in 1 Timothy), give us clues to keeping proper balance in our relationships with those who compose our work.

The minister's relationship with parishioners may be understood through a variety of analogies. They are coworkers, the fruit of our labor, providers of godly counsel, and friends, just to name a few. Ultimately, our "work environment" or the "fruit of our pastoral labor" are actual people, created in the image of God and part of God's own family. It is not as if our work is about simply producing a product. Nor is our work to add numbers to our attendance rolls. Ethicist and philosopher Immanuel Kant's reminder to treat people as an end in themselves, and not simply as a means to an end[6] echoes Jesus's Golden Rule, which instructs us to treat others as we would be treated. Furthermore, we are to treat others as valuable in the sight of God and not simply as tools to be used for our own ends. That being the case, we must keep in mind key ethical elements in our relationships with parishioners.

First, our work relationships should never have pride of place over our relationships with God, self, family, or mentors and friends. These relationships outrank job or job-related relationships. However, what happens when our job is to engage people—not products or services—with the love of God? The fact that our *job* is to share the ongoing good news of Jesus Christ through *relationships* with people is precisely what makes it difficult for pastors to maintain clear priorities.

This brings us to a second key ethical element in maintaining healthy relationships with parishioners. The nature of our work involves being available, developing genuine concern for those under our care, and dealing with people at the most intimate and vulnerable places of their lives. Recognizing that this is part of our calling and job description, we must create and maintain both boundaries and accountability in order to maintain proper balance so we can be successful over the long haul.

## RELATIONSHIP SIX: COMMUNITY

Regardless of the size of the community, the title *pastor* or *minister* carries certain expectations. This dates back to early Catholic practice, still in place, of dividing spheres of a local church's influence into parishes. As a key representative of the church to the community, the minister is tasked with presenting both a witness for Christ and the church as a welcoming place for others. The minister also has the opportunity to serve as a voice for the community to the congrega-

CRITICAL RELATIONSHIPS IN MINISTRY

tion, especially the voices of those who are underrepresented or who have special needs. On a practical level, involvement in community food pantries, chaplaincy, and ministerial alliances are ways the minister can be a bridge builder between the church and community.

Ethically speaking, this priestly kind of role for the minister follows the model of Jesus, who was often a voice to the religious people of his day on behalf of the overlooked, the forgotten, and the downtrodden. Jesus cleared the temple in anger at the religious community's greed and their willingness to make it more difficult for Gentiles to worship at the temple (Matt. 21:12-17 and parallel accounts). Jesus chastised the well-to-do, who looked down upon the poor or upon women or upon other outcast groups. Jesus became a voice of comfort for those who felt overlooked by the religious community of his day. These are just a few of the reasons why community involvement by the minister is part of an important ethical relationship with others. The minister and the leaders of the congregation should enter into up-front agreements regarding the place of the church, and specifically the minister, in the community. These agreements should take seriously the priorities mentioned already, and they should be clear enough to avoid resentment or misunderstanding on the extent of the minister's role in the community.

Of course, as Eugene Peterson reminds, there are always challenges when the minister and the church engage the community around them. The language of business or politics can easily replace the language of theology and of compassion. The church and the minister may indeed become "community activists" in a way that allows the church to speak to the political and economic issues in the name of Christ; however, the church and minister must remain a voice of Christ-centered theology. Our language and approach should reflect Christ-like ideals of peace, justice, and reconciliation shared in love, not the often cold language of business or the accusatory language of politics.[7]

The ways in which we partner with the community around us, including the way we do business in the community, determine whether or not the church will remain a prophetic voice of change and care or simply become another voice that furthers the status quo.

## MEASURING SUCCESS IN RELATIONAL TERMS

The movie *A Civil Action* is based upon a true story, in which onetime ambulance-chasing attorney Jan Schlictmann loses nearly everything when he takes up the cause of families who have been poisoned by the toxic waste produced by a large corporation. Schlictmann becomes convinced through interactions with affected families in the small Northeastern community that he should devote all of his time and the resources of his small law firm to assisting them in suing the two polluting corporations for damages. The battle drove Schlictmann's firm to bankruptcy. In bankruptcy court, the lawyer poses this question to the judge: "Where did it all go? The money, the property, the personal belongings . . . the things by which one measures one's life? What happened?" As the lawyer sits in silence, we hear distant sounds of families and children—the clients for whom he gave up his comfortable living.

The real Jan Schlictmann later reflected on the experience, saying that losing everything was one of his life's most enriching experiences because it emptied him of things that once made his life shallow and allowed him to embrace a deeper meaning of success. This is very much a model of success in Christian ministry, according to Jesus: "For whoever wants to save their life will lose it, but whoever loses their life for me will find it" (Matt. 16:25). This is not to say that all ministry leads to poverty. Rather, success in ministry is rarely measured in the same way that success is measured in other professions. Our definition of success has more to do with ethics in our relationships than with the objective measures that define success elsewhere.

Will D. Campbell was a white minister from Mississippi who became one of the leading civil rights activists of the twentieth century. Reflecting upon his earliest opportunities to preach, he recalls that the first book he was given was not about theology or even preaching methods but about how to overcome shyness. He mused that even at that early stage, he was surprised that "such practical and social habits as that seemed more important than what I might believe about one theological point or another." He adds, "Interesting that I should find the same thing true throughout years of theological training. The training was for success, not faithfulness to Christian theology."[8] Training for ministry, at its best, has traditionally been countercultural in regard to its approach and content. When we focus our preparation mostly on how to achieve the numerical or monetary measures of success that we have borrowed from the world of business, we fail to train ministers to judge themselves and their ministry by the one measure that truly matters—the ways of Christ.

Reinhold Niebuhr is perhaps the best-known American ethicist of the twentieth century. Before becoming a leading ethical voice and later president of Union Theological Seminary in New York City, Niebuhr was a pastor in Detroit during a tumultuous time in American history, the late 1910s and early 1920s. Niebuhr's journal from that period, titled *Leaves from the Notebook of a Tamed Cynic*, is as informative to pastors as most of his later works in the formal study of ethics. In one entry, written in 1921, Niebuhr writes about being introduced as a guest speaker to a gathering of businesspeople from the Detroit area. Niebuhr noted that the speaker mentioned that he was lauded as "a pastor who had recently built a new building at the impressive cost of $170,000." Niebuhr found it interesting that, in this gathering of businessmen, the only way the speaker felt the best way to recommend him was as an able businessman himself. Niebuhr noted, "That would have given the good men of my church council a laugh."[9] Niebuhr goes on to state that he was thankful that "there is no quarterly meeting in our denomination and no need of giving a district superintendent a bunch of statistics to prove that our ministry is successful."[10] Earlier in his ministry, Niebuhr had lamented, "It isn't easy to mix the business of preaching with the business of making a living and maintaining your honesty and self-respect."[11]

These examples are in no way meant to deny the importance of reaching people, preferably a great number of people, in the work of ministry. Nor are they a validation of the stereotypical view of the minister as impoverished. However, when it comes to measuring success and excellence, we face an ethical struggle due to the contrast between Scripture's measurement of faithfulness and the world's fascination with numbers and riches. In fact, it is easy to confuse biblically based ministry success with the ability to draw people and raise large amounts of money. Those who opt for the latter at the expense of the former struggle against the prophetic foundation upon which the church is constructed. No wonder a growing number of retiring or retired ministers look back upon their life's work—work that, for some, included large churches and copious amounts of funds raised—with a sense of emptiness and regret. It appears that many climbed a ladder of success that was leaning against the wrong structure.

These examples remind us of the need for a different way to measure what is good, what is right, and what is successful. Giving in to nonbiblical definitions of these concepts compromises the integrity of our faith and witness as well as our ministry priorities. My first district superintendent once said that if we grow the largest church in the denomination but lose our families or lose our own souls, we have lost everything. Using the ways of Christ to define success and goodness keeps us from losing our way.

To create that better way of measuring success, it will be helpful to understand the distinction between *norms, morals,* and *ethics.* A social norm is a set of behaviors that become part of the cultural landscape. Social norms originate from various places, including prejudice or simple convenience. These norms are "the way things are," which means that they are not always good and that communities rarely make ethical judgments about them. They are habitual actions or ways of being that the community has adopted over time.

Morals are the societal, cultural, or organizational norms that are deemed to be good. These morals have not always been subjected to a systematic evaluation, but they have been deemed good by a consistent majority of the group over time. Ethics is a system of determining right or wrong based upon the elements discussed in chapter 1: having an authority, taking seriously the community, and with a systematic means of consistent evaluation.

When measuring success, it is tempting to simply accept the norms and morals of the culture in which we live. For instance, some towns have clear boundary lines between races that are considered normative, although they are no longer legally enforced. That is a norm that has been left relatively unchallenged and unchanged over time. Violating a norm or moral in a given community can create controversy for a minister but can also provide an opportunity to promote a Christ-centered, prophetic message to the community. Applying a biblically based ethical system and consistently teaching and promoting such a system can challenge the norms in a given setting. This should be done with a loving attitude from the minister and the church.

Measuring success in ministry is not a matter of appropriating the norms or morals either of the surrounding culture, the community, or other professions. To measure success in ministry requires the development and consistent application of a Christ-centered ethic—that is, a system for determining what is good based on the ways of Christ and in concert with the church. What the community of faith deems to be "success" will not always result in immediate praise from the culture. However, by changing definitions of success and being a consistent agent in allowing a Christian ethic to challenge moral norms that are unchristlike, the minister authentically demonstrates healthy priorities and fosters a new definition of success. Again, this may cost the minister in the short run, since even other ministers and ministerial leaders may be reluctant to confront a norm or a set of morals in a local church or in a community. Yet we are ultimately responsible before God to uphold the ethic of love exemplified by Christ himself.

## Mentoring Questions

1. What tools do you use in your own life and ministry to assist you in keeping your priorities properly aligned (these "tools" can include other people, such as mentors)?

2. Explain the relationship between a having Christ-centered definition of success and consistently keeping one's priorities. How are they related?

3. Give examples of times when you have made sacrifices in order to maintain healthy priorities in your relationships. Pray for continued success and accountability in these areas.

## Suggested Reading

Niebuhr, Reinhold. *Leaves from the Notebook of a Tamed Cynic.* New York: Literary Classics Library, 2015.

Nouwen, Henri. *In the Name of Jesus.* New York: Crossroad, 1992.

Peterson, Eugene. *The Contemplative Pastor.* Grand Rapids: Eerdmans, 1989.

# 4

# COMMUNICATION,

# THE LIFEBLOOD OF MINISTRY

"Pastor, would you kindly remind her that Ephesians 5 says that she is to submit to me as she submits to Christ!" This is how the counseling session with a couple in my first pastorate began. As I sat there stunned, looking at this man's wife, whose eyes quickly dropped to the floor, I realized that it did not take a great deal of training to recognize the red flags in this case. The woman began to cry and to protest that her husband never listened to her real issues. He retorted that he always listened but she never respected him or his decisions. Chaos quickly ensued. After regaining their attention, I pointed out to the man the difficulty with the passage he had cited: it contains an instruction for husbands too! Since he seemed unaware of that, I asked him to read that portion of

Ephesians 5 aloud: "Husbands, love your wives, just as Christ loved the church and gave himself up for her" (v. 25). This became a clarifying moment for him that eventually led to the couple getting some much-needed help. Their communication had been decidedly one-sided: he spoke, made excuses for his behavior, and quoted a convenient portion of Scripture to his wife, while she refused to consistently share her feelings or even to confront him.

Communication is the lifeblood of relationships. Unhealthy communication kills relationships. Unfortunately, widespread communication problems in a congregation are not easily remedied. The powerful tongue, which is compared to a rudder of a ship in James 3, can indeed turn congregations of all sizes away from health.

Throughout Scripture, God is a constant communicator, always trying to connect with those whom he has created and seeks to redeem. The garden of Eden narrative in Genesis 1–3 portrays God as speaking all things into being. Even after the disobedience and deceitfulness of Adam and Eve, they still "heard the sound of the Lord God as he was walking in the garden" (3:8), as was apparently his custom. God is never swayed in his attempt to communicate clearly and effectively. He speaks to chosen men and women in regard to Israel, so that through Israel all nations may be drawn into the conversation (see Gen. 12). When even more clarity is needed, God comes in the person of Jesus Christ, whom John's Gospel calls "the Word" (John 1:1). God not only speaks but also listens. He hears the cries of his people (e.g., Pss. 18:6; 120:1). God even dialogues with outsiders, such as the Samaritan woman (see John 4). God is both a consistent talker and the consummate listener. The creator and sustainer of the world also creates and sustains healthy dialogue. This is likely why many of the psalms are psalms of lament or complaint: God listens, even when we complain about the direction in which his universe is going.

Communication is an important aspect of God's character, and it is a vital part of the work of a Christian minister. This chapter focuses on the minister's role as facilitator of healthy communication within the church.

## COMMUNICATION TROUBLES

"You never told me that!" This statement is commonly heard in families, in the workplace, and in church life. Another common accusation, "You don't understand me," also makes frequent appearances during times of church conflict. It is frustrating when what is said is not interpreted as intended. Also frustrating are those times when the meaning is indeed heard but sparks disagreement. Perhaps worse than either of those are the times when no genuine communication is attempted at all. By genuine communication, I mean the kind of dialogue in which two or more parties have opportunity to speak, to be heard, to clarify, and to respond honestly and without fear. Genuine communication falls by the wayside when parties push a one-sided agenda in a dictatorial or bullying manner, when there is no opportunity given or taken to respond, or when people regress to a point of not communicating at all. Personal agendas, strained relationships, and weary communicators are just a few of the obstacles we face when trying to communicate honestly, openly, lovingly, and clearly with each other. How can we as ministers of the gospel follow God's example in creating healthy dialogue amid so many barriers?

## AN EARLY ATTEMPT TO COMMUNICATE EFFECTIVELY

When I came to my first pastorate, I had just started seminary, just gotten married, and faced a board that had seen the church through trying times in which communication had all but dried up. Many of my board members had grandchildren older than I was. Most of the rest had children my age. The situation was intimidating to a brand-new twenty-three-year-old pastor. My mentor told me that I needed some rules of the road for communicating with my congregation. How would I get people so much older than I to talk to me rather than among themselves?

I drew up a list of rules that evolved into ten principles that have transformed the way our church communicates. They now form a covenant signed each year by all the leaders, including me.

1. If you have a problem with me, come to me privately.
2. If I have a problem with you, I'll come to you privately.
3. If someone has a problem with me and comes to you, send the person to me. I'll do the same for you.
4. If someone consistently will not come to me, say, "Let's go to the pastor together. I am sure he will see us about this." I will do the same for you.
5. Be careful how you interpret me—I'd rather do that. On matters that are unclear, do not feel pressured to interpret my feelings or thoughts. It is easy to misinterpret intentions.
6. I will be careful how I interpret you.
7. If it's confidential, don't tell. This especially applies to board meetings. If you or anyone comes to me in confidence, I won't tell unless (a) the person is going to harm himself or herself, (b) the person is going to physically harm someone else, or (c) a child has been physically or sexually abused. I expect the same from you.
8. I do not read unsigned letters or notes.
9. I do not manipulate; I will not be manipulated; do not let others manipulate you. Do not let others try to manipulate me *through* you. I will not preach "at" you

on Sunday mornings. I will leave conviction to the Holy Spirit (he does it better anyway).

10. When in doubt, just say it. The only dumb questions are those that don't get asked. We are a family here and we care about each other, so if you have a concern, pray, and then (if led) speak up. If I can answer it without misrepresenting something or breaking a confidence, I will.

Sometimes after we'd agreed on these guidelines, a couple of church members asked a longtime member of the church to "tell the pastor" about some idea that they felt was not working. At first, this leader agreed to speak with me. Then, she called the two members back and said, "I've thought about what you asked me to do. I know that the pastor would appreciate it if you told him yourself. He always wants to hear what church members think. If he does not respond, then call me and you and I will go together."

That afternoon, the members sat with me in my office, and we worked through their problem. At the time, I did not know that the longtime member had sent them to me. "I'm so glad you came to me personally," I said at the close of our conversation. "Around here, all of our leaders believe in open communication, even about difficult matters, and we have agreed to try and communicate with each other this way."

Later, when I learned the rest of the story, I knew our adherence to this kind of healthy communication had given the leader an opportunity to communicate her confidence in me. And I was allowed to cement two other relationships that might have presented roadblocks later on.[1]

These ten guidelines have been reproduced in a number of book chapters and articles since their initial publication in 1999.[2] They are also used in many local churches and at least one Episcopal diocese as required covenants of communication. The reason for this is not that these principles are new or innovative. Rather, it is because consistent communication is the key to healthy relationships, and every healthy relationship begins with up-front boundaries and agreements that set the tone for long-term growth.

## COMMUNICATION KILLERS

As the years progressed in my first pastorate, I learned in more detail why this agreement became an important part of that church's life. The main reason is that it directly addressed problem areas—things I began to call *communication killers*—in our church. Communication killers are approaches to communication that short-circuit the process of communication before it has a chance to get started. And since communication is the lifeblood of an organization, these communication killers can be church killers as well.

Early in the history of the church, the church councils addressed areas of theology that affected the long-term theological health of the church. The creeds, the final statements of the councils, ensured that the church would proclaim the gospel with clarity. Those who could affirm the key creeds of Christianity would no longer continue to teach doctrines contrary to the basics of the Christian faith (*heresies*). So a new Christian could not declare at baptism that he or she affirmed that Jesus Christ is truly God and truly human and still hold to heresies claiming that Jesus Christ was not human but was a kind of spirit being who only appeared to die. The creeds became safeguards against "killer doctrines"—heresies that would weaken or destroy the Christian faith.

In a similar way, up-front agreements about how we were to communicate with each other set a healthy tone that rid our congregation of the communication killers that were destroying it. Here are some examples of communication killers that can be rooted out by establishing clear ethical agreements about communication.

## Avoidance

The easiest and perhaps most prevalent way of dealing with conflict is not dealing with it at all. This technique is called *avoidance*, and it will come as no surprise that there are very few cases where it is either effective or ethically sound. The dangers in avoiding conflict are at least twofold. First, avoidance of conflict can give the impression of implicit approval of unhealthy or unethical behavior. As Martin Luther King Jr. once wrote regarding Christians who failed to speak up concerning civil rights: "He who passively accepts evil is as much involved in it as he who helps to perpetrate it. He who accepts evil without protesting against it is really cooperating with it."[3] The second danger of avoidance is that it can give the appearance of apathy toward people or important situations that arise in church life. It should be noted that there is a difference between avoidance and hesitation or even delay in addressing certain areas of conflict. "Fools rush in," as the old saying goes, and there are times when the healthiest option is to wait: to wait on God's timing, to wait until there is further investigation, or to wait for tempers to cool down, for example. But this waiting is the postponement, not avoidance, of honest and healthy conflict. Waiting should never be an excuse to avoid a difficult conflict or ethical dilemma.

## Passive-Aggressive Communication

An old comic strip depicts a church member greeting the pastor in the church foyer with a scowl, and the caption reads: "I shared all of this information with you last week, and you had to go and preach on sin! I'll never be able to trust you again!" The parishioner in the comic likely feels personal conviction for sin, which he just happened to talk about with the pastor. However, the comic reminds us of the dangers of passive-aggressive approaches to communication.

Passive-aggressive communication involves communicating either too indirectly or in a way that singles out a person or issue without directly addressing it. That's the passive part. The aggressive part usually follows, when the communicator, after trying to give subtle hints that are not received or acknowledged, resorts to direct and often angry or overdramatic communication in marked contrast to the earlier, cryptic approach. Long-term passive-aggressive communication can lead to fear, resentment, and mistrust. It also creates an environment in which decisions must be based upon assumptions or trying to read between the lines instead of clear and open communication.

## Lying

This communication killer is likely the most obvious. Since early childhood, most of us are taught to tell the truth. We are also taught that dire consequences follow when lies are told and spread. Even so, the temptation to lie is great, even in ministry. The generally accepted ethical definition of a lie has two parts: it must misrepresent reality or truth, and it must have the intention of practicing deceit, usually for a selfish purpose. What are ways in which ministers are tempted to misrepresent reality with the intent of selfishly deceiving? Attendance statistics, schedule commitments, and educational achievements are common areas where lying creeps into ministry. The pressure we feel to present an image of growth and competence can make intentional misrepresentation appealing. Blaming others—including other staff members—for our own errors is another temptation that can catch ministers unprepared.

Counselors often say that "we are only as sick as our secrets." Lying is a type of secret keeping that impedes intimacy because it creates an environment of suspicion, fear, and mistrust. Even in our preaching we can foster an environment of dishonesty by attributing experiences in the sermon to ourselves that were actually borrowed from someone else.[4] An environment of distrust is an environment in which intimacy cannot flow, and it can falsely indict the church, which is supposed to represent the truth of Christ in the world, as a place of dishonesty, no different from some secular institutions.

## Triangulation

Early in my pastorate, Sally and Mike (not their real names) came to me with marital difficulties. After explaining to them that I was not a marriage counselor but would be happy to talk with them as a pastor and refer them to a counselor if needed, we arranged to meet. Soon Sally began coming to church more and more, while Mike was less visible and, according to Sally, was increasing his consumption of alcohol. One afternoon Mike showed up at my office. He had obviously been drinking, and he complained that Sally had locked him out of the house the night before. He then proceeded to tell me that Sally was not the person she pretended to be, and that she was verbally and even physically abusive to him and, at times, to their two children. I was shocked and disappointed. I was so disappointed that I found myself siding with Mike in the marital struggle, though I did not condone his drinking. When Sally called me a couple of days later asking if I had seen Mike, I told her that I had seen him and that I was disappointed in her actions toward him and her children. I had taken Mike's word to be true. She began to cry and lashed out at me for betraying her trust and taking the word of, in her words, that "drunk and abusive man."

Over the next two weeks, I spoke with both Mike and Sally separately, playing go-between, sometimes reporting to Mike some of Sally's perspective while at other times doing the same for Sally. I felt comfortable doing this because I believed my own perspective would be more objective and even more diplomatic than their own. After a few weeks of this, the two of them showed up together at my office. I smiled, believing that my work as ambassador had paid off in restoring a troubled marriage. That was not the case. For the next several minutes, they took turns expressing their disappointment in me for betraying their confidence and of "interfering" with their personal lives. They left in anger, telling me that they would be finding a new place to worship. I never saw them again. Over time, and after inquiries to my wife (a trained counselor) and some mentors, I recognized the mistake I had made as an unhealthy form of communicating called *triangulation*. Triangulation is a phenomenon that occurs when two people or entities in conflict utilize a third party to avoid direct confrontation with one another. Triangulation is a substitute for direct and healthy communication among parties who have conflict.

What should I have done differently? I should never have become a go-between in this situation of intense conflict. As one Christian counselor reminds, when anxiety increases in any system (such as a church), relationship triangles are likely to result, and pastors need to be able to differentiate themselves from the unhealthy emotional baggage that comes with entering into an unhealthy triangle.[5] This is difficult because, as pastors, much of our theological identity is wrapped up in mediation: we have a "priestly" role that involves helping others to hear God's voice more clearly. However, there are healthy and unhealthy ways to mediate. Triangulation is an unhealthy way since it relies on hearsay and indirect communication, which far too often is misinterpreted. Also, triangulation keeps issues and responsibilities fuzzy, in the words of pastor and counselor Ronald W. Richardson, which confuses the roles and responsibilities of those involved in conversation and conflict.[6] Our mediation should clarify, not confuse.

## Bullying

Authority, as we have defined it, involves a conscious choice to grant something or someone sway over our actions and/or attitudes. Power-based authority, while most popularly identified with the word *authority*, is actually the weakest form of authority, since it changes one's actions and attitudes by force and they easily revert back when the power or force is removed. Bullying is communication that seeks change based on the use of power, and the influence of bullies, as is the case with all force-based authority, depends on the consistent presence of the bully. When a bully is removed from the picture, his or her influence disappears and healthy communications are free to flow.

The problem, of course, is that church bullies tend to stay around because they are rarely confronted. They generally prey upon weaker members of the church, and others are afraid to confront them. In other settings, these relatively silent accomplices are called *lackeys* or *toadies*, and they sometimes join the bully, under the bully's protection, in coercing others. That happens in churches as well. Well-known Christian writer Thom Rainier lists nine characteristics of church bullies that include gathering tidbits of information and shaping it to their own agendas.[7] Since church bullies often have self-serving agendas couched in a stated intention to "save the church," it is difficult to pin down their true motives and clearly confront them.

A preventative maintenance approach to dealing with bullies begins with a clearly stated theological vision and mission for the church, accompanied by consistent modeling of healthy communication. This allows leaders to pinpoint specific actions perpetrated by a bullying person or group within the congregation and to confront it in love. Oftentimes, bullies detect a positive change in the health of the local church and choose to leave voluntarily. Of course, their leaving is often accompanied by a good deal of blaming and accusing others—especially those in leadership—about changes in the church.

The danger for pastors in confronting bullies is two-fold. First, it is likely that bullies have built relationships with enough of the congregation to keep themselves protected for a long time. For some congregants, sadly, "friendship" or some version of it outranks their theological or ethical convictions. They fear confronting and alienating a so-called friend, even if that friend happens to be a church bully.

Second, bullies tend to develop a self-centered focus that renders them immune to the logical or even emotional appeals for compromise that are effective with most other people. Bullies often count on the fact that no one will resort to the kind of directness they have mastered over the years in order to stop their bullying. Sadly, they are often correct.

Therefore, a pastor can find himself or herself dealing with a crisis like the one faced by a fictional town marshal in the classic movie *High Noon*, in which a group of bullies that the marshal had arrested years earlier come back to town to run him off or gun him down. The marshal struggles to confront these bullies when virtually the whole town, including his own deputy, has chosen to abandon him out of either fear or apathy. Like this marshal, who chooses to stay and stand up to the bullies, the pastor must sometimes determine whether to confront a bully who controls a church by coercion so that the congregation can be a Christ-centered community of grace and compassion. All ministers have stories that go either direction, for there are times when the congregation's willing-ness to maintain the status quo is stronger than its willingness to confront unbiblical behaviors. The minister can either com-ply, thereby becoming a lackey for the bully (which happens far too often and is often considered "success" by observers) or stand up and risk moving to another assignment or losing a great deal of support. Jesus chose to stand up to bullies, and it cost him his life. Jesus did bring about the conversion of some bullies though; and when local churches see this kind of victory, it opens the door for long-term health, even if it costs short-term attendance and giving.

I know of a church leader who confronted a church bully who happened to be one of the strongest givers in the church. This bully was also a faithful church attendee, though he alienated many and hurt several members to the point of causing them to leave. The new pastor, after about a year had passed, confronted the consistent behavior of this person. The church bully did not leave but did contact many of his "friends" (those who tolerated the bullying behavior and were afraid to confront it) and informed them that he would no longer contribute funds to support this pastor who, in his words, was "alienating key members." Despite this bully's unwillingness to give, the church's income actually increased by 10 percent over the next nine months.

Unfortunately, this is not always how such encounters end. Bullies sometimes gain short-term victories. Pastors, key leaders, and even those who oversee clergy can easily become lackeys, either willingly or unwillingly, in order to maintain the short-term viability of the church. At such times the pastor has to maintain his or her ethical integrity, to confront in love using a biblically based approach, then make the choice to remain in the church or leave it based upon the direction the congregation chooses. The pastor's authority, like all authority, is a granted authority. If the congregation refuses both biblical and clergy authority, moving on may be the best option. However, when a bully can be converted to using healthier approaches to communication, it sets a positive, redemptive example to the entire congregation. And if a bully does decide to leave and even draw some people with him or her, the congregation is then free to make long-term changes in its methods of communication. Some call this "growth by subtraction," and Jesus's own ministry validates this reality. When healthy communication leads some to leave a congregation, it is crucial to remember the distinction between the biblical definition of success and worldly definitions (such as higher attendance or giving) and to act with integrity. Several passages of Scripture record people leaving Jesus: religious leaders (e.g., the Pharisees in Matthew); potentially big donors (e.g., the rich young man in Luke 18); some who were troubled by Jesus's teachings (e.g., John 6:66); and those who could not control Jesus or get their way (e.g., Judas Iscariot), some even through bullying (cf. the arrest of Jesus in John 18). Jesus was saddened by these departures, and he continues to love those who have been harmful to his cause. But Jesus never gave in to the pressure of bullying. Consequently, the kingdom of God did not always grow with great speed, but it did grow with great integrity.

## ELECTRONIC COMMUNICATION

The prevalence of electronic technology, particularly social media, has revolutionized communication. It has expanded the horizons and the scope of communication, which has been both positive and negative. Positively, mass communication is time saving and far reaching, giving even the smallest of congregations the potential to create a truly global presence. Negatively, most cyber communication includes no way to read the tone of a conversation, and it is much easier to send thoughtless, emotion-based, reactionary responses at the touch of a button. Such responses can greatly alter the health of a church. Words once spoken can never be taken back. And in the electronic age this is even more relevant, because words published on the Internet never truly disappear. Furthermore, they can be shared over and over again! Therefore, in utilizing the communication benefits offered by the Internet, a minister is wise to employ rules of etiquette, which may include allowing time to pass before responding to an electronic message, consulting with others about the potential impact of an electronic communication, and using face-to-face communication rather than electronic communication for sensitive matters.

## Summary of Electronic Communication Etiquette

In the light of the cautions listed above as well as the prevalence of electronic communications in all of life, here are a few quick reminders that can prevent misunderstandings or rash behavior in electronic communications in ministry:

1. Do not say anything electronically that you would not say face-to-face. *Electronic communication gives a false sense of anonymity that can cause one person to speak to another in inappropriate ways.*

2. Remember that tone cannot be "read" in an electronic communication. *What one person means as frivolous may be read on the other end as negative or hurtful. Experts remind us that authentic communication relies on nonverbal cues. Those cues are not present in electronic communication.*

3. Use electronic communication to facilitate face-to-face communication. *It is usually wise, especially in complicated matters, to use electronic communication as a tool to schedule face-to-face interactions ("Can we discuss this matter on this day?") and to follow up on face-to-face discussions ("To review, I heard us say . . . during our meeting. Is that how you saw it?").*

4. If extended electronic communication is necessary, re-read, edit, and even rely upon a different (and trusted) set of eyes than your own when possible. *Although electronic communication is fast, real communication takes time, work, precision, and editing. Before sending an important electronic message, especially one involving conflict, prayerful editing and even reliance on a trusted person to read and*

*interpret what you are trying to say can avoid unnecessary communication in the long run. A little extra time "up front" for electronic communication can ensure clarity.*[8]

## Mentoring Questions

1. Discuss a time when you experienced one of the "communication killers" in the church.

2. What are some benefits of a communication covenant like the one mentioned in this chapter? What are some potential challenges in implementing such a covenant?

3. How would you describe this distinction between success as understood through the lens of Christian ethics and a more general definition of success? In what specific ways have you seen this distinction lived out?

## Suggested Reading

Carter, Les, and Frank Minirth. *The Anger Workbook*. Nashville: Thomas Nelson, 1993.

Richardson, Ronald W. *Creating a Healthier Church: Family Systems Theory, Leadership, and Congregational Life*. Minneapolis: Augsburg Fortress Press, 1996.

Scazzero, Peter, with Warren Bird. *The Emotionally Healthy Church*. Grand Rapids: Zondervan, 2010.

# 5

## DEALING WITH

## CHURCH CONFLICTS

Simply having a set of agreements in place does not prevent unhealthy communication. There must also be a loving, yet direct, way to address people who refuse to abide by the agreed-upon guidelines. Agreements of this nature are not to be used in a manipulative or even legalistic fashion. In fact, a gentle reminder, reinforced by other leaders in the church, is often all it takes to set a new tone of healthy communication throughout the congregation. Regardless of the preventative maintenance we put in place, troubles will still come. As Jesus said, "In this world you will have trouble" (John 16:33).

Those who make intentional, Christ-centered preparation for ministry will encounter conflict, as will those who do not make thoughtful preparation. The difference is that those who are intentional about creating a healthy, proactive ethical environment will be better prepared when (not if) the conflicts come. The Communication Covenant in the last chapter, for example, will stop some conflicts before they occur if people are aware of and committed to its basic communication boundaries. Even when some refuse to comply, an up-front agreement or covenant provides a basis for addressing conflict. Tools like that one can help bring conflicts to a clear resolution. With this in mind, here are some key concepts of communication for dealing with conflicts in ministry.

## THE ROLE OF ANGER IN CONFLICT

"In your anger do not sin," the Bible reminds (Eph. 4:26). I like the King James Version better in this case, since it is more direct and more adequately reflects the emphasis of the sentence in the Greek: "Be ye angry, and sin not." Conflict can arouse anger in one or both parties. Anger is a natural response to threats or fear, both of which arise in many conflicts. Not all anger is bad, though some Christians have mistakenly thought so. Jesus himself got angry (see Matt. 21:12-17). However, in the words of Christian counselors Les Carter and Frank Minirth, there are both productive and nonproductive ways of being angry. The nonproductive way uses anger to manipulate or control, which produces long-term grudges and acts of aggression toward those who disagree.[1]

Anger can be useful when it motivates us toward clarity in communication or enables us to see the need for either self-improvement or improvement of the environment in which we find ourselves.[2]

Many churches would be healthier today if a pastor, lay leader, or even a district leader would have gotten angry and directed the anger toward the issue or the behavior of a person or group instead of falling victim to one of the unhealthy communication patterns mentioned in the previous chapter. Too often we ignore, or, worse yet, "promote" those who are causing conflict. By *promote* I mean that we tend to give troublesome people more responsibility, hoping this will either appease them or keep them busy enough that they don't hinder what we are trying to accomplish. This is unhealthy and unethical: it rewards behavior that is contrary to the stated purposes of Christ and his church. "Do not promote your problems," a longtime Methodist leader once said. Promoting problem people instead of confronting them directly and lovingly reproduces their behavior in others.

Some churches would be healthier if their leaders and members did not use anger to justify *all* behaviors. Often, a moment's relief can cause months or even years of difficulty when a minister does not weigh his or her words before speaking in anger. When this happens, confession and forgiveness are essential for the health of the relationship.

Anger drives us to seek quick resolution to a conflict, and that is sometimes the best approach—but not always. The balance of deontological concerns (choosing what is right regardless of the consequences) and teleological concerns (that which results in the best outcome) must drive our decision-making regarding how *and when* to engage in conflict. Issues that rise to the level of being right regardless of the consequences should be addressed consistently and quickly. Even if we are right, of course, we are still called to address the conflict in the most Christlike way possible, leading with love and concern and not self-righteousness or punitive motives. At other times, a conflict may be of lesser priority, and those involved can take more time for evaluation before jumping into the fray. "Be as shrewd as snakes and as innocent as doves" (Matt. 10:16) is an apt motto for these occasions.

Some conflicts are simply not worth dying for, especially if they do not greatly hinder the mission of God and the church. Other conflicts demand an immediate encounter, and putting them off only compounds the problem. Some areas of conflict—especially those that involve straying from the theological and missional norms of the church—should be addressed clearly, even if it would be more politically expedient to let them go. For other areas of conflict, a wide range of approaches and solutions, including compromise, may be the best way to preserve the integrity of the church and to resolve the issue.

## BASIC KEYS TO ETHICAL CONFLICT RESOLUTION

Scripture shows us that the men and women portrayed therein are not superhuman. Even the "heroes of the faith" had flaws—often glaring flaws. Those flaws often provoked conflict and confrontation. Since conflict among God's people is inevitable, ministers must be prepared to address it in an ethical manner. This list of basic keys for dealing with conflict represents the best of many approaches to healthy conflict resolution in the church, taking seriously the need for preventative maintenance.

### 1. Establish Healthy Boundaries Up Front

Church members must have biblical boundaries for communicating together, especially in regard to conflict. This is sometimes called *metacommunication*, or communicating about communication. Working together before conflicts arise about how communication is generally going to occur in the church allows for clear communication when inevitable conflict arises. (See Appendix A for a sample Communication Covenant.)

### 2. Concentrate on Actions, Not Personalities

While in the midst of a conflict is not the time to try to completely change the personality or attitude of another person. The first priority is to address behavior. So, instead of saying, "You are selfish and rude," which deals with abstract personality traits, address the behavior only by saying something like, "When you did/said _____, I/we felt _____." Or, "This action is contrary to our agreed-upon policy."

## 3. Listen and Clarify

Along the way, it is often useful to stop and clarify. You can do that with a question like this: "You said _____. My interpretation of that is _____. Is that a correct interpretation?" Clarifying communication sets the stage for a clearer resolution and agreements later on.

## 4. Seek Clear Resolution and Agreements

Remember, the goal is not to shame the other side or to claim "victory." The ultimate goal in addressing any conflict is growth in Christ and greater health in the church. That means that after both sides have been represented and heard, it is time to seek resolution based on the up-front covenants and ethical boundaries of the church. Seeking this kind of resolution prevents the church from making an arbitrary decision based upon popularity, power, or favoritism. Once the behavior or decision in question has been evaluated in light of the church's up-front covenants and ethical boundaries, the parties can make an agreement on how to (a) make amends for personal harm, and (b) move forward with a new approach that is more in line with the values of the church.

## 5. Practice Accountability and Follow-Through

Once agreements are in place, leaders must practice loving accountability to ensure that agreements are consistently carried out. Periodic check-ins with those involved in the conflict—not to rehash the past, but to evaluate and celebrate progress in moving forward—is essential. If agreed-upon expectations aren't being met, further resolution may be needed. In some cases, that could involve outside arbitrators who can reinforce the church's desire to settle matters in a Christ-like manner. Sometimes people who are held accountable choose to leave the church. The Bible reminds us that this is not a new phenomenon. In these cases, the fact that one or more parties have left the church does not negate the agreements made, and those agreements must be consistently and lovingly enforced even if one or more of the parties returns much later. The integrity of the church's approach at this point will set the tone for the resolution of future conflicts.

## LOVE, NOT FEAR

"Perfect love drives out fear," as the Bible reminds (1 John 4:18). Too often, however, the process of conflict resolution is controlled by fear, usually reactive fear. This often creates greater conflict and allows unresolved issues to linger. Worse yet, power-based or politically based attempts at resolution may be made, setting an unhealthy precedent for future conflict as threats, power plays, and bullying become the norm. However, rooting conflict resolution in the love of Christ and his ways sets at least three important precedents.

First, it creates an environment in which the goal is not simply to appease key individuals but rather to create a resolution that furthers the ways of Christ. Second, although all conflict can create tension, that tension is lessened when conflict is handled with clear communication and when all parties involved—regardless of who is ultimately deemed right—conform to the ways and spirit of Christ. Third, it creates an environment where health and restoration are emphasized over shaming or demonizing, leaving room for the many good things that Scripture promises for those who love, even in times of conflict.

## Mentoring Questions

1. What is your reaction to the word *conflict?* Discuss whether or not your reaction is generally positive or negative and why.

2. Discuss a difficult conflict you have experienced or heard about in a church setting. Critique the way it was handled (by you or by others) based upon the insights of this chapter.

3. Discuss a few of your own "to die for" issues. Does that discussion result in either the addition or subtraction of items from your list?

## Suggested Reading

Dana, Daniel. *Conflict Resolution.* New York: McGraw-Hill, 1991.

Meier, Paul. *Don't Let Jerks Get the Best of You: Advice for Dealing with Difficult People.* Nashville: Thomas Nelson, 1995.

Sande, Ken. *The Peacemaker.* Grand Rapids: Baker Books, 2004.

# 6

# THE ETHICS OF

# PASTORAL CARE AND COUNSELING

"Pastor," the distraught wife began, "we are desperate." As she and her husband sat in the pastor's office, their countenance showed cold detachment. "Our relationship has been so steeped in anger, bitterness, and poor communication that we are near the end. But before we consulted a lawyer, we wanted to give it one last shot, so that is why we are here today."

That scenario is far too common. Few couples are quite as honest as the one mentioned here, but if we were to peel back the facade of normalcy that many married people display, we would hear similar words. In fact, by the time most couples get to the pastor's office with their issues, it is often too late, or at least time is running out. This is not a statement of cynicism but an observation of the lack of preventative maintenance in many marriages. Couples often enter marriage with strong feelings of love and affection but little preparation for dealing with the inevitable conflicts and changes of environment they are about to face. Furthermore, in a culture rife with divorce, few couples witness healthy models for dealing with conflict, so they bring very few tools for relationship growth into marriage. Pastors often feel that they are trying to stop a tidal wave when counseling couples in serious marital conflict. It is as if the husband and wife have lost control of a semitruck and are asking the pastor to please stop their vehicle from plunging over a cliff.

Thankfully, there is hope in Christ, and that is indeed what we offer. However, this hope comes through a multilayered process that involves both the pastor's voice and many accompanying voices over an extended period of time. Before looking further into the ethical boundaries of pastoral counseling, let us look more generally at a key area of pastoral ministry that is often overlooked, though it can be an indispensable aid in establishing a healthy environment of preventative maintenance: pastoral care.

## PASTORAL CARE: SHEPHERDING THE FLOCK OF GOD

Keeping watch over the flock evokes thoughts of the Christmas story: this is what the shepherds were doing before the annunciation of the birth of Christ by the angels. Yet there is more to this task. Keeping watch is the ongoing work of shepherding for which pastors are responsible. Thomas C. Oden calls shepherding a "pivotal analogy" for understanding the pastoral role.[1] Keeping watch is not serving as the congregational watchdog, scouring households for signs of immorality. Rather, keeping watch is the ministry of presence that fosters an environment of healthy growth and communication in the church. Oden summarizes the function of pastoral care, patterned after the approach of Jesus (see John 10) in the following way. It is knowing the parish territory, developing a sense of trust within the congregation, anticipating the needs of the congregation through intimate knowledge of them, as a group and individually, as one who is consistent in both teaching and presence. In short, Oden reminds that the role of the pastor as shepherding caregiver is "no incidental, take-it-or-leave-it image for ministry. Consistently it remains the overarching analogy under which all descriptions and functions of ministry tend to be embraced: the good pastor, whose vigilant caring is an expression of Christ's own eternal caring."[2]

As longtime Christian psychologist Larry Crabb writes, ongoing and connective care, not just from the pastor but from all in the congregation, can serve a preventative function as well. In his book *Connecting*, Crabb reminds us that our relationships within the church can be sources of healing, since "the unbearable reality" of our disconnectedness from God and from others is the source of so many of our problems.[3] Certainly, the ministers of the congregation, as leaders, take initiative in this: in providing opportunities for communication, whether in informal and seemingly meaningless interaction or in serious matters of life and death. Both extremes, and those conversations in between, are incarnational ways of sharing in the journey of the kingdom to which God has called all of his children. Christ's call to Peter to "feed my sheep" out of love for Christ is extended to us all as we minister in the church of Jesus Christ (see John 21).

Long-term caregiving provides avenues for deep interaction. Those who trust our ongoing care will also trust us with crises that arise. At such times we must evaluate the best possible route to provide that care for those who have asked for our help. Sometimes, this involves extra and intentional interaction: giving spiritual direction at a crossroads in life. At other times, we ministers rely upon partnerships developed with other trusted professionals to see that parishioners receive the best available care in their hour of need. Here we turn to the most pressing of ethical considerations regarding pastoral care: What are the limits of our own training and availability in situations that require long-term therapeutic and/or medical solutions? Some suggestions regarding boundaries follow.

## Recognize the Limits of Your Training

"I tried a new thing yesterday," the young pastor said to his counselor friend over coffee. "I tried the empty-chair technique." The counselor friend looked surprised.

"Where have you heard of that?" he asked.

"Well, I was introduced to it briefly in a course in college, and then we discussed it briefly in a pastoral counseling course in seminary. I have always been intrigued by it. When this young woman came in with unresolved issues with her dead father, I thought it would finally be the perfect time to give it a try!"

"What happened?" the counselor asked.

"I told her to imagine her father sitting in the chair and to have an honest conversation with him about anything that had been unsaid in order to start the overall healing process," the pastor said as he reclined in a self-satisfied smile, expecting congratulatory praise from his counseling colleague.

Suddenly the counselor leaned forward. "Did you schedule a follow-up? Did you moderate the conversation with appropriate cues? Did you reflect upon some of the long-term goals that arose from that outpouring of emotion?"

"Well, no," the pastor said shyly. "But she did say that she felt better afterward and that she was glad she finally got to shed tears over her father's death and over their relationship. It seemed very healing for her."

"No!" exclaimed the counselor. "You witnessed what may be the *beginning* of healing, but not healing. Using the empty-chair technique in isolation is like giving a painkiller to someone with a broken arm! It will make the pain go away, but it doesn't fix the deeper issue." He added, "You will be lucky if that experiment doesn't deepen her problem and her depression in the long run. If I were you, I would refer her to longer-term help immediately." After slamming a tip on the table, the counselor got up and left, leaving a deflated pastor who realized that he had overstepped his level of training.

That is not an uncommon scenario in ministry. Pastors honestly desire to assist, and we are flattered and even humbled that individuals or couples in need come to us to bare their souls and to share their most intimate areas of concern. However, it is incumbent upon the pastor to seek help in determining which approaches assist in a pastoral counseling and which are best reserved for longer-term therapeutic counseling. Doing so can mean the difference between providing a bandage to a person who scratches a hand on a doorknob and doing an appendectomy on someone who has appendicitis! In other words, overstepping the limits of our expertise in regard to mental illness or emotional distress can have comparable consequences to overstepping one's medical training.

Ministers can take advantage of local and denominational resources to enhance their counseling technique, and some even opt for clinical pastoral education while serving as a pastor in order to acquire more training and tools for pastoral counseling. Even ministers with clinical psychological training and mental health certification are wise to recognize the time commitment required in an ongoing therapeutic relationship. Pastors trained as counselors or therapists may wish to weigh their role as therapist against the larger responsibility of the pastoral care needs of the entire congregation. After doing so, they may wish to refer those in need of therapy to another professional. Regardless, a responsible minister stays within the boundaries of his or her training and is ready to refer and come alongside in a complementary way when the needs of a parishioner exceed the abilities of the pastor.

Ministers should be equally cautious about giving advice in other areas where special training is required. Giving advice or practicing outside of one's discipline, job description, or training is a form of malpractice, a term usually associated with physicians but one that is becoming used more often for professions such as Christian ministry.[4] Other areas of ministry malpractice include:

- **Giving medical advice** ("I wouldn't take that pill if I were you!"), if the minister is not a practicing physician and the physician of record for the parishioner.
- **Giving legal advice** ("Here is how I think you should handle your criminal proceedings"), unless the pastor is a practicing attorney and the attorney of record for the parishioner.
- **Giving financial or investment advice** ("You should definitely purchase stock in Company X if you want a solid return"), if the pastor is not a certified financial adviser.

The position of influence we have been given by the very nature of our role as ministers suggests—both ethically and, in many states, legally—a type of expertise. When we give advice in areas outside of our area of training, we risk giving a false impression that can result in harm to our parishioners. As long as we clearly state that we are solely giving our opinion in such matters, if we choose to speak about them at all, and as long as we are clear that we are *not* speaking as a lawyer, doctor, or financial adviser, we protect both the parishioner and ourselves from misunderstanding and misrepresentation.

## Be Honest about Your Schedule

Author and counselor Howard W. Stone of Brite Divinity School argues that offering short-term pastoral counseling is

a healthy practice for all ministers.[5] Sticking with brief therapeutic relationships, Stone argues, helps prevent the abuses
that can occur in long-term therapeutic relationships because
it discourages dependence upon the minister as the source
of healing. Stone concludes, "Short-term pastoral counseling thus minimizes the chances for abuses of power and, in
the parish context, allows pastors to continue ministering to
parishioners after counseling has ended."[6]

Long-term therapeutic relationships with parishioners
may exceed the pastor's available time, resources, and skill
level while depriving the rest of the congregation of pastoral
contact. Communicating clearly about the limits of our availability for pastoral counseling opens the door to conversations
about referral to a therapist if needed, and allows the pastor
to shepherd parishioners toward the healthiest solutions.

## Keep Confidences

"I have something to tell you, Pastor." Conversations that
begin this way, whether in casual interactions with parishioners or in pastoral counseling, may involve anything from
life-changing victories ("We're having a baby!") to heartbreak-
ing tragedy ("My mother has cancer"). Devoting oneself to
the nurture and care of others means participating in the
ups and downs of life along with them. We "rejoice with those
who rejoice" and "mourn with those who mourn," as Scripture
says (Rom. 12:15). When we are granted access to sensitive
information from people to whom we minister, we also receive
certain responsibilities. Most often, we are not viewed as a conduit for passing along news. Instead, we are seen as a trusted
sounding board who will lend a trained and caring ear. This
creates an implicit agreement to maintain confidentiality.

In an earlier chapter, we examined a Communication
Covenant for churches that includes the statement "If it is
confidential, I won't tell." The covenant adds exceptions for

information about abuse of a minor or the elderly, or the sharer's intention to harm himself or herself or others. In such cases, the covenant shared in this book makes no guarantee of confidentiality. This is partly due to the fact that laws in nearly every state require ministers to report such information to the authorities. Furthermore, pastors have an ethical responsibility to protect those who are the most vulnerable in our society and to reasonably prevent imminent harm to others. In nearly all other cases, including confessions of other types of past wrongs or crimes, most ministers are bound to secrecy by virtue of their ordained or licensed status. However, as spiritual advisers, we are also obliged to urge those who need to make confession or to correct a wrong to do so. However, this rarely, if ever, means that we should reveal something shared in confidence.

In a growing number of states, provisions are in place that protect ministers from the coercion to testify concerning nearly all matters shared in a pastoral counseling or a spiritual advisory setting. Each minister has a moral obligation to know both the limits of the law in the state or country in which he or she is serving as well as the limits and standards of confidentiality afforded by one's own denomination.[7] Ministers should be aware that there may be times when the confidentiality requirements of one's denomination conflict with the law. In other words, there may be times when maintaining the confidentiality demanded by one's denomination puts a minister at odds with secular authorities. This could put the minister in a precarious position if subpoenaed to testify in court.

Up-front communication upon entering a pastoral counseling relationship with a parishioner will avoid confusion in these matters. For instance, a document stating the limits of the minister's training and time and the limits of pastoral confidentiality could help create a healthier counseling environment. For instance, I know of a case where a grandmother witnessed what she thought was physical abuse of her grand-child by her son-in-law. She was reluctant to report the matter, given the close family ties, yet she was genuinely concerned about the health of the child. She approached her pastor one evening before a worship service in the following way: "Pastor, I would like to talk with you about a concern I have regarding my grandson and his father." The pastor pulled her aside into his office and quickly replied, "I am willing to talk with you about anything, and I realize that what I am about to say may not apply to what you are going to share with me. However, if I have reason to believe that a minor has been abused, I am required to report it to the secular authorities."

"I understand," the grandmother replied. She then shared her entire concern, including two actions that both the grandmother and the pastor deemed abusive.

The pastor said, "I understand your concern, and I will pray about it. I will also make a phone call in the morning."

"Thank you," the woman responded.

In this case knowing the limits of confidentiality actually assisted the grandmother in doing what she could not bring herself to do. This resulted in intervention by child protective services that protected the child from further harm. The fact that the pastor had made known his approach to confidential-ity gave this grandmother the tool she needed to do what was most helpful for her grandson and daughter.

## Be Honest about Potential Moral Pitfalls

In an early interview with *Time* magazine, world-re-nowned evangelist Billy Graham noted one of the ways he maintained safe boundaries while traveling frequently away from his wife. Stating what has come to be known as the Billy Graham Rule, the evangelist said that he never has a meal alone with a woman. In his autobiography, Graham mentions that he applied this rule even to heads of state, once turning down an invitation to a one-on-one dinner with a first lady of the United States.[8] Interaction with persons of the opposite sex is unavoidable in ministry, whether in casual conversation, staff meetings, routine pastoral care, or pastoral counseling. Therefore, it is essential to determine boundaries up front, such as the so-called Billy Graham Rule, before awkward situations arise.

For many years Graham's rule was taught to and adopted by ministers almost without question. However, new concerns regarding its necessity and effectiveness have made it the subject of debate, especially in denominational settings and in local churches that allow for mixed-gender pastoral staff. Opinions vary regarding the rule's effectiveness and necessity. Should this strict limitation apply to males and females who are on staff together and who therefore frequently interact over meals or coffee? Does this rule represent the repression of sexuality that may actually encourage more temptation to immorality? Does the rule present an unfair and unnecessary barrier to a more inclusive ministry in the church for both males and females?

Either way, engaging in routine pastoral care or extended times of pastoral counseling across gender lines calls for healthy boundaries. Love-based rather than fear-based approaches provide a healthier environment for genuine interaction and potential healing. One of our objectives as pastoral caregivers is to be transparent, loving, and honest. On the other hand, such transparency can easily be misunderstood or misapplied, leading the minister to cross ethical boundaries. The result can be destructive to both pastoral trust and the minister's reputation. Here are three important considerations for creating up-front ethical guidelines for mixed-gender contact in a ministry setting.

## 1. Theological Considerations

The Bible emphasizes that both males and females, as created in the image of God (Gen. 1:26-27), have equal value in God's sight. Men and women are both essential in the spread of the kingdom of God, as we note in Jesus's reliance on women in the spread of the gospel (e.g., the Samaritan woman at the well in John 4, Mary Magdalene in John 20, and Mary and Martha in John 11). Paul also references women as co-laborers in the gospel (e.g., Priscilla in Rom. 16:3). Therefore, pastoral boundaries should take seriously the equal value of males and females, and we should be reluctant to assume the worst when approaching the opposite sex in a counseling situation. Creating a hard-and-fast rule (a strict deontological approach) does not take into account every situation. Neither males nor females who offer pastoral care or counseling should assume that the other party is going to "come at them" in a lustful way just because the minister offers an empathetic ear. At the same time, using discernment regarding times, locations, and consistency of interaction is crucial in order to demonstrate respect for one another and for the entire congregation, including our spouses.

## 2. Relational Considerations

We should give attention to the hierarchy of voices that participate in setting our ethical boundaries. For example, the spouse of a married minister may be wary of or feel threatened by certain members of the opposite sex. Taking seriously the concerns of a spouse in setting boundaries for cross-gender pastoral care demonstrates respect for the spouse and can provide a healthy pattern for future interactions. This does not mean that all counseling between the genders should be avoided. However, honest spousal interaction regarding boundaries will allow for the minister to offer care and counsel while avoiding potential pitfalls.

### 3. Accessibility Considerations

Ultimately, we must balance the need for equal access to pastoral care and counsel by people of either gender while demonstrating a healthy respect for the ethical integrity of all relationships affected. There will be times when women and men must interact in pastoral situations where other members of their gender are not present. In those settings, transparency is the key. While confidentiality is a sacred trust, confidentiality does not imply a lack of transparency in regard to intergender counseling and care interactions.

In conversations with female ministerial colleagues and with my wife (formerly a practicing therapist), the words *discernment* and *relationships* are mentioned.[9] Discernment regarding the motivation for and frequency of pastoral interaction is imperative. A healthy question before entering into a pastoral counseling or care situation is: What motivates my desire to give counsel or care? Am I acting out of genuine, loving concern, or are there ulterior or self-centered motives that draw me toward this person or situation?

Transparency and accountability help prevent straying toward unhealthy interactions with parishioners, whether or not a counseling session is involved. Being honest with yourself and accountable to others will help you discern if or how to apply the Billy Graham Rule in your ministry. The relationships involved, especially relationships with spouses, must also be taken into account. Scheduling numerous counseling sessions with a person with whom the minister's spouse is uncomfortable can demonstrate disrespect for the minister's marriage. Likewise, if the counselee is seeking to use the minister as an escape from or replacement for his or her own marriage relationship, extreme caution is needed and counseling sessions should be minimized or even avoided. These considerations apply to all counseling and pastoral care relationships. Pastors should keep confidences, but that does not include hiding the fact that a pastor is spending inordinate time with a particular parishioner. Secrecy is not the same as confidentiality.

Rather than creating a hard-and-fast rule, based on fear, that restricts pastoral interaction between the genders, it may be best to rely on informed discernment, key relationships of accountability and commitment, and transparency to determine the goals and frequency of interaction.

### Refer Responsibly

In his book *The First 100 Days*, Scott Daniels reminds pastors that an important part of beginning a new pastorate is assessing available community resources. This includes resources for counseling referral.[10] The pastor should counsel only within the limits of his or her training and job description. As theological leaders of the congregation, our role as pastoral counselors is to assist in the practical application of Scripture to individuals and families who find themselves in need of relationship help. This does not mean that we simply quote relevant Scripture to them, of course. It means that we engage in the kind of dialogue that connects them to a deeper relationship with Christ and points them toward his care in the midst of their struggles. We do this in every realm of life, but we do not assume that this is the only help our parishioners need. Rather, we realize that pastoral care and counsel are the foundation parishioners need to move toward healing. Once we have laid this foundation, we may often need to refer parishioners to other professionals who can assist in more specific areas of health and healing. For example, we can provide comfort, care, prayer, and biblical encouragement to a church member who is experiencing ongoing pain. However, it would be irresponsible to limit that member to this aspect of healing alone. The responsible thing to do would be to refer the person to a trusted physician who could provide medical treatment.

Likewise, for parishioners who may show signs of mental illness, emotional distress, or long-term personality disorders, it is incumbent upon ministers to provide prayer, care, comfort, and biblically based encouragement while also encouraging the parishioners to seek more specific psychological treatment. Historically, ministers have been more likely to refer the parishioner with physical pain to a physician than to refer a parishioner with mental, emotional, or relationship pain to a mental health professional. However, both ethically and legally, the stakes are higher than ever regarding the need for responsible referral in cases that exceed the minister's training and expertise.

How does a pastor choose a suitable mental health professional to whom he or she can refer those placed under his or her pastoral care? Recalling the Ethics Grid and relationship priorities addressed in the earlier chapters of this book, we see that the pastor must weigh the balance of Christian values and recognized training when evaluating referral sources. These questions may help identify those sources.

- Does this counselor profess a faith in Jesus Christ, and how does this faith influence his or her approach to therapy?
- Is this person certified in accordance with the laws of the state in which they serve? Are they active members of organizations within their profession that practice consistent and proven approaches to therapy?
- Are they willing to meet with the minister to discuss general approaches to counseling and therapy?
- What is their standard rate or fee, and do they have a sliding scale arrangement? Do they accept payment from insurance carriers?

Once you make a list of competent mental health professionals in your area and begin to refer, recognize that it is unethical—and often illegal—for the therapists to directly share details of their therapy sessions with you. However, you may assure your parishioners that you can meet them consistently to follow up on their progress, encourage them, and offer support for putting what they learn in therapy into practice. In this way, pastoral care and counseling complement the work done is a therapeutic environment and give the parishioner the best possible care in the long run.

All pastors should make available to parishioners both a list of competent and trusted mental health professionals for those who require more than a few sessions of pastoral counseling, and a written statement of the benefits and the limits of the pastor's approach to pastoral counseling. Conversations with mental health professionals will reveal where their own counseling boundaries are and when a referral should take place. A sample document can be found in Appendix A.

### Encourage Help for the Journey

Regardless of the extent of one's counseling training, as those who shepherd God's flock, we ministers can confidently direct those in our care to the best available assistance while continuing to play a vital part in their journey toward wholeness. Preventative maintenance will create an environment in which it is easier for those who are struggling with issues that require more than a short conversation or even a few pastoral counseling sessions to ask for and receive help. Creating a healthy environment begins by setting healthy ethical boundaries, counseling within the boundaries of the minister's training, maintaining healthy confidences, and establishing relationships with competent Christian mental health professionals with whom we can partner.

## Mentoring Questions

1. What elements do you think are important to include in a pastoral counseling policy?

2. Discuss your own limitations in regard to counseling and therapy.

3. Discuss how you might develop a resource list that includes trained therapists in your community.

4. What are your denominational and personal limits in regard to confidentiality? How have you, or should you, communicate them to your congregation?

## Suggested Reading

Crabb, Larry. *Connecting: Healing Ourselves and Our Relationships.* New York: HarperCollins, 2005.

Minirth, Frank, and Walter Byrd. *Christian Psychiatry.* New York: Fleming Revell, 1990.

Oden, Thomas C. *Pastoral Theology: Essentials of Ministry.* New York: HarperCollins, 1983.

Rowell, Jeren. *What's a Pastor to Do?* Kansas City: Beacon Hill Press of Kansas City, 2004.

Savage, John. *Listening and Caring: A Guide for Groups and Leaders.* Nashville: Abingdon Press, 1996.

# 7

# HANDLING

# THE BUSINESS OF MINISTRY

"The love of money is a root of all kinds of evil," the Bible reminds (1 Tim. 6:10). Perhaps only sexual immorality has caused the downfall of more ministers than the mishandling of money and improper business practices within the church. The following scenarios present ethical problems that pastors encounter every day. As you read them, briefly begin to formulate ethical and tactful ways to address them.

- A volunteer who has been consistent and faithful in attendance and giving intentionally opposes the initiatives of the pastor and the church leadership, using his influence to undermine the direction of the church.
- A board member is exerting influence on church leaders to choose her company as its insurance provider, even though her rates and coverage are not the best available.

- A paid church nursery worker who is consistent and reliable with children asks to be paid under the table, meaning that she does not want her income reported to the IRS.
- A staff member who was hired years before the new pastor arrived consistently refuses to follow the directions and policies now in place and is using his influence to undermine the new pastor's ministry.

These are versions of business-related issues that affect churches every day. We have already addressed healthy communication principles, upfront communication agreements, and conflict resolution. All of those, to some degree, come into play in dealing with difficult business situations. However, these matters also involve the business practices of the church. How can the church handle money ethically, including how we spend that with which we have been entrusted? Can volunteers be dismissed? Are there effective ways to hire and even fire paid staff members? What workplace standards should set the church apart even from the strict workplace standards that exist in the world of business?

To address these issues requires a serious commitment to the ethical standards we have already discussed. It also requires vigilance and commitment to resist the temptation to co-opt the practices of business or politics rather than that indicated by Christian theology and ethics.

## PRINCIPLES OF ETHICAL FINANCIAL MANAGEMENT

The Parent-Teacher Association (PTA) is an important organization that has a variety of affiliates across the United States. This organization exists to support local schools in achieving their goals with personnel and resources from the community. The PTA is not the school and does not set the vision for the school; it merely provides resources. Finances are an important resource in ministry, but they are no more and no less than a means to a greater goal. Just as the PTA serves as a key support in achieving the mission of a school, the finances of a church must support its overall mission. Therefore, the handling of finances should command the time and attention of every minister, especially in regard to three key areas, which for our purposes can be described with the acronym PTA: personnel, transparency, and accessibility.

A transgression in one or more of these areas can indicate an ethical violation, which endangers the trustworthiness of the ministry and jeopardizes its future funding. Worse yet, red flags raised in these general areas can signal a violation of state or federal laws, which can affect not only the trustworthiness of a ministry but also lead to legal consequences for the minister and church leaders.

## Personnel

Who is handling the church's finances on a weekly basis? Even in smaller congregations, ministers and other leaders should be intentional in determining who collects, counts, records, and reports on the giving in the local church.

## Transparency

Transparency in regard to finances is not only a smart practice for building trust but also an ethical responsibility when handling monies given to promote the mission of God in the world. The troubling story of Ananias and Sapphira in the book of Acts is not a story about a couple who were struck down because they did not give all or enough. Rather, it is a story that illustrates that a lack of transparency—in their case, lying publicly to the church about the amount they have given—is equivalent to lying to the Holy Spirit (see Acts 5:3). One would be hard-pressed to find a contemporary example of ministers or other leaders being struck down for lack of transparency in regard to finances (thank the Lord!), but transparency remains a sound ethical principle for dealing with finances. This transparency includes integrity in handling dedicated funds—gifts given for specific purposes in the church.

## Accessibility

Accessibility is the final part of our triad of financial red flags in church life. The local church should strike a balance between preventing access that would hinder confidentiality or cause favoritism for certain givers and allowing enough accessibility to giving records to prevent the consistent misuse or misappropriation of church funds. A senior minister should always have full access to all giving records and must therefore guard himself or herself from allowing such knowledge to lead to favoritism toward those to whom he or she ministers.

## GUIDELINES FOR ETHICAL FINANCIAL MANAGEMENT

Those entrusted with oversight of church finances should have a strong and consistent system of managing their own personal funds. This does not necessarily mean that those who are successful in business or who are personally wealthy are best suited to oversee church funds. The church must ask more probing questions of those entrusted with financial management because our standards of success differ from those of the world. An unethical wealthy person can be just as destructive to the reputation and mission of a church as an unethical person who lacks wealth. We can extend the application of Paul's admonition to Timothy in regard to church leadership to church financial management as well: if one cannot manage his or her own household well—in this case, including one's personal finances—that person should not be entrusted with church funds (compare 1 Tim. 3:4-5). Selections like this must be handled with proper discretion and discernment; however, it is a recipe for disaster to entrust financial oversight to someone who either has made money in a questionable manner or who uses his or her financial position as a means of control or who does not manage his or her personal finances well.

The church must resist the temptation of what Christian business ethicist Alexander Hill calls *dual morality*: allowing the culture of business to shape our ethics in a way that is contrary to the holiness and love of God.[1] You may recall the line from the classic movie *The Godfather*, in which Michael Corleone says to his brother, "It's not personal, Sonny. It's strictly business," as if the two realms of relationship operated by entirely different moral codes. When it comes to sound principles of business in the context of church life, we may be tempted to separate our Christian ethics from the expediency of "doing business," thereby sacrificing a key area of Christian witness. One need only read the headlines in recent decades to see that duality in regard to how we do business as the church—financial management, hiring and firing decisions, proper use and accounting of monies—has caused great mistrust among those who observe us.

These guidelines, gathered from a variety of denominational sources, will serve any church well in regard to money management:

- Ask probing questions regarding how someone came into wealth and whether he or she is willing to work within the congregation's financial guidelines and under the direction of the pastor and church board before appointing that person to financial office.
- Ministers should not handle church monies directly without others present. Use support staff for this purpose, who are approved by the governing body.
- Ministers should not be check signers. Delegate this responsibility to approved parties in the congregation.

All checks should be signed and distributed only within the framework of board and budget approval. These approval guidelines should be written and should be agreed upon up front.

- Evaluate at least monthly the financial reports of your church. For most congregations, this is accomplished in a monthly board or congregational meeting. The pastor should be aware of the financial trends and budget status at all times.
- Establish up-front accountability guidelines for the use of staff credit cards. Credit card purchases that fall outside the approval guidelines should be reimbursed to the church by the party who made the credit card purchase. This reimbursement *cannot* be counted toward annual giving.
- Use an IRS-approved accounting system for expense reimbursement. Most denominations provide reimbursement forms that can be used in a local church.
- Use financial teams for greater accountability. This includes a team for counting money, a team for reporting, and a team to whom each authorized spender is accountable. This reduces the temptation to make the finances of the church the subject of gossip, misunderstanding, or misinformation.
- Focus giving appeals on the mission of the church. J. Clif Christopher reminds that a key reason people give is to further the aims of the church, not simply to meet its operational costs. "To sum it up," Christopher writes, "people want to be a part of something that changes lives."[2] Gary McIntosh and Charles Arn echo this: "People give more to pursue vision than to pay bills."[3] This does not mean that we should be dishonest about real needs or emergencies. In fact, transparency is the key to strong and ethical giving. However,

the focus of our giving is upon who we are: we are the church, and our mission is to further the work of Christ in the world. Reminding people that they are not simply giving to another nonprofit, are not giving in order to get recognition, and are not giving to promote a message they control is the key to Christian giving. When we give, we give to the mission of Christ. We entrust a portion of our income to the one who provides all of our income by his grace. We are not "self-made" people: we are people of grace, and when we give to a church that is defined by the mission of Christ we both promote change and are changed.

- Specifically address the needs of all givers without playing favorites. In his book *Not Your Parents' Offering Plate*, Christopher argues that treating all givers equally is a mistake that churches make in their fundraising.[4] The variety of age-groups present within most local churches—builders, baby boomers, Gen Xers, millennials—all have different motivations in regard to giving, and if pastors are not attuned to these realities, our appeals for giving will likely fall on deaf ears.[5] "Don't even waste the paper on sending a WWII [giving appeals] letter to a Gen Xer," Christopher writes.[6] The good of this statement from an ethical perspective is that genuine pastoral care involves translating the gospel and its mission into a variety of languages, cultures, and age-groups. That isn't just smart from a pragmatic point of view, it is also a genuine reflection of the way Jesus approached those whom he taught. One need only note the parables of Jesus to see Jesus's knack for translating across these kinds of lines.

    Christopher also urges pastors to appeal in special ways to the wealthy givers in their congregations. He clarifies his point by stating, "The argument I hope you hear being made is that the rich need the attention of their pastor to know how to handle the burden of money."[7] This, rather than treating the rich as any more special than the poor, should be the focus of the church. God revealed himself the most clearly through poverty: the Incarnation occurred in the context of an impoverished family from an overlooked and oppressed minority community! Surely we should not forsake those through whom God presented his clearest message of grace. However, if we approach wealthy parishioners as Jesus did the rich young ruler—loving them enough to call them to an identity higher than that of his riches (Luke 18:18-30)—we preserve the balance between appreciating their generosity and calling them to be accountable for their use of wealth within the kingdom of God.

- Dedicated funds must be used as directed. This, like many financial issues, carries both a legal and a moral obligation. In most cases, it is illegal to use funds directed to a particular project or area of ministry to fund a different area. Of course, it is also unethical. Also, remember that a governing board may refuse to accept funds that are directed for a purpose not in line with the mission of the congregation. For example, if someone wishes to donate a used vehicle and receive a giving receipt for tax purposes, the church has full authority and even an ethical responsibility to (graciously) refuse such a gift if it would simply sit on church property and collect dust. This kind of discerning decision-making keeps the focus of the church's giving on the mission of the church. I know of many instances where a church graciously refused a special gift because the giver was using the "special designation" gift as a means of controlling the church's agenda or of decluttering his or her own house. Discernment is part of good stewardship.

## ACCESS TO FUNDS AND INFORMATION

At least two people should be present for counting money and should not include the pastor or members of the pastor's family. The counting team should include more than two persons, and they should rotate. Counters should be trustworthy, consistent, and able to keep confidences. Their role is to count and record the results. Use of a reporting form that includes the names of the giver and the gift assists the church in keeping track of giving for the annual giving reports required by the IRS. These reports should be distributed by January 31 for the preceding year. The names of givers should be kept in a secure place in order to maintain confidentiality. Those who should have access are: the pastor, the treasurer, and at least one member of the counting team (sometimes called a financial secretary).

Some pastors are uncomfortable looking at giving records, though some pastors are required to sign annual giving receipts (usually along with the treasurer or church board secretary). Some members also balk at giving the pastor access to this information. However, two key factors emphasize the absolute necessity of pastors having consistent access to these records at all times. First, it is a matter of pastoral care. As one mentor said, "If couples in your congregation are having relationship troubles, you are expected to know, even though this is an intimate detail. Likewise, the intimate detail of financial consistency should also be part of your care." This is not a matter of showing favoritism, and pastors should guard any temptation to show favor just because someone gives more than another person (see James 2). However, since, as the saying goes, the wallet is often the "last thing laid on the altar," being aware of giving patterns is key to pastoral care. Changes in giving patterns can be a sign of economic or relationship struggles that can be gently addressed by pastors who are aware of the need. Furthermore, many churches require that a person be a consistent giver in order to be elected or appointed to certain leadership positions; therefore, knowledge of consistent giving patterns is necessary in making informed decisions regarding leadership.

The second reason why knowledge of individual giving patterns is important for pastors is two-way accountability. Ultimately, pastors are responsible for the fiscal well-being of the congregation, and any audit of church finances will involve interaction with, among others, the pastor of the congregation. Therefore, it is not only morally but also legally irresponsible for a pastor to be unaware of giving patterns of members or for any members of the congregation to bar pastors from access to such records.

As in every other relational or spiritual matter in the church, pastors must maintain proper confidentiality and abstain from favoritism regarding the giving of church members. However, these cautions should never prevent pastors from exercising proper accountability, not only in the overall financial health of the church but also in the giving patterns of individual members entrusted to their care.

## ETHICAL CONSIDERATIONS FOR VOLUNTEERS

"You can't *fire* volunteers," said the well-meaning church secretary to a young pastor who was discussing a plan for dealing with unhealthy ministry patterns in her local church.

"Yes, you can," the minister replied. "And sometimes you have to." As with every aspect of church business, the approach to such "firings" differs significantly from the approach in a secular business environment. For instance, relieving a volunteer of a burdensome ministry with which he has been "stuck" for years may evoke gratitude from the one "fired"! In ministry, most terminations of responsibility should actually be changes of positions, from a place where the volunteer is not gifted or excited to a place where he or she is more qualified and passionate. This is more than just practical advice, although it has practical merit. It is also an ethical principle. Everything we do in the kingdom of God is a gift. The talents, the opportunities, and even the needs for personnel are gifts of grace, and the needs are to be filled by those who have the gifts, graces, and the willingness to fill them. Furthermore, unlike the corporate world, it is often better in the church to have many people doing the job of one than it is for one person to do the job of many. Jesus seems to have a very different definition of *efficiency*, as many of his parables illustrate. For example, think of the parable of the sower (Matt. 13:3-9), who scattered seed about in a way that no farmer today would describe as efficient.[8]

One ethical conflict that both pastors and church volunteers face stems from the church's concept of service, which differs greatly from the idea of a "volunteer" in other nonprofit organizations. Disciples of Christ throughout history, even those who were entrusted with ministry oversight (i.e., vocational ministers) have "left everything" to serve the work of Christ (see Mark 10:24-31). We are all volunteers, in that sense. Popular notions of volunteerism emphasize the charitable sacrifices and contributions of those who serve without pay. The church has always acknowledged the value of those who give and serve sacrificially. However, in most other organizations, the term *volunteer-driven* can mean *volunteer-controlled*. In other words, it is not uncommon for volunteers in certain types of organizations to be "more equal than others" in the sense that those who give more time and money or have more wealth exert more influence within the organization than those who give less. Furthermore, most volunteer-driven organizations see volunteers as exempt from many (though not all) of the requirements expected of those who are paid. That means a volunteer can often pick and choose—within certain boundaries—how committed he or she will be to the overall mission and vision of the organization. The organization is simply thankful for whatever small, large, or sporadic contribution a volunteer makes—there is no deeper accountability.[9]

We in the church should indeed be grateful for large and small contributions of time and resources. But this is where the similarities break down. The church's call to service is an echo of the call of Jesus Christ himself: a call to surrender our will and our control to the leadership of the Holy Spirit expressed through the body of Christ, the church. This distinction is crucial because each person who becomes part of the church becomes an ambassador, a representative of the entire church and its mission. As Paul writes, "We are therefore Christ's ambassadors, as though God were making his appeal through us" (2 Cor. 5:20).

This means that the church has higher expectations of its volunteers than do most volunteer-driven organizations. The placement of workers in the church is a serious matter requiring us to walk a line between the desire for maximum involvement by laypeople and the mandate for all Christians—not just paid ministry staff—to exemplify a consistent walk with Christ, especially when entrusted with any position in church life. This consistent walk includes commitment to the structure and mission of the church. We are people under authority: the authority both of Christ and of those whom Jesus and the church have put in places of oversight. All Christians, then, whether paid or volunteer, must not serve in ways simply to entertain or benefit themselves. Rather, all serve under the authority of Christ and of his ways.

This means that we are not driven to increase our numbers by having a large corps of volunteers when those volunteers do not accept the authority of Christ and his ways. Recruiting a larger team is a worthwhile result that often follows a healthy approach to ministry; however, it is a secondary goal. The primary goal is to enlist volunteers who promote the ways of Christ in the church, community, and the world and who are in harmony with the theology, polity, and leadership of the church. Having these kinds of expectations means that, unlike many volunteer organizations, the church's recruitment standard involves more than simple availability, talent, or resources. These three things are important, of course. However, those who do not seek to fulfill the higher calling to Christian service within the context of the church should not be entrusted with positions of influence. Also, those who are talented, available, and financially well off yet do not exemplify the harmony and consistent witness of a mature Christ follower can and should be removed from positions of leadership, even if they are volunteers.

When the rich young man mentioned in the Gospels (Mark 10, Matt. 19, and Luke 18) went away sad after refusing Jesus's invitation to sell all of his belongings and give to the poor, then follow Christ, the disciples were shocked: "Who then can be saved?" they asked (Mark 10:26). Seeing the higher standards the church places upon the role of volunteers, one may be tempted to ask, given those standards, "Who then is fit to volunteer?" Thankfully, God does not demand absolute perfection from any of us who serve in ministry, whether paid or volunteer. However, the minimum standards are quite high: growing in Christlike character, willing to be held accountable, consistent in the giving of both time and resources, and seeking to work in harmony with the church's mission and its leadership. These are higher standards than in many volunteer organizations. Perhaps church life is the only place where volunteers are asked to dedicate not only their time but also such a high degree of loyalty to the overall mission and to act in many ways as if their life and their living depended upon the work they do for Christ through the church.

Commitment to the person and work of Christ—the theological and ethical boundaries of our mission—makes someone a viable candidate to work in church life, even as a volunteer. The sacrifice involved in such an endeavor transforms the worker and builds the body of Christ. The willingness and humility to do this work are gifts from God. Jesus reminded the bewildered disciples, who were dismayed that one so wealthy and talented was apparently turned away because his wealth and talent were higher priorities than following Jesus, that not all who are talented, wealthy, and willing need to be lured away: "All things are possible with God" (Mark 10:27).

## ETHICAL CONSIDERATIONS FOR PAID STAFF

### Hiring

Traditionally, ministers and churches have been reluctant to use the word *hire* when it comes to ministry. This is likely because of Jesus's stern contrast between a true "shepherd" and a "hired hand" in John 10:12, who, "when he sees the wolf coming, . . . abandons the sheep." This is indeed an important theological distinction to make when employing someone in a ministerial capacity. Beyond that, there are other important legal and ethical issues surrounding the employment of anyone in a position of oversight.

The dual responsibility of the minister hiring staff is to the future staff person in creating the best possible transition into a place of trust and to the organization in giving the church confidence in the hiring process and the qualifications of the staff person. Therefore, even in situations where a church gives sole hiring responsibility to one person, transparent dialogue and strong advice and consent are necessary to create a sense of trust. Furthermore, transparency with the candidate about expectations and the hiring process is crucial for forming a strong and lasting staff relationship.

## Firing

What happens when the employment relationship no longer works for the church? As in any other professional environment, we in the church must be aware of both legal employment policies and ethical considerations in the termination of employees. Recently a minister successfully sued a denomination after being released from his congregation. This minister had an agreement with the denomination and with the local congregation that was not honored. The minister, who had tried to make things work despite the denomination's and congregation's unwillingness to fulfill the financial agreement, eventually resigned. Rather than being forthright about their inability to meet agreed-upon terms, church leaders implied in a public church service that the minister had misappropriated church funds and had therefore resigned. The result: the district and congregation lost a suit that cost them over $300,000.[10] Just as nonreligious businesses are expected to approach both hiring and termination with transparency and in keeping with the law, so must churches.

Churches and other nonprofits often have written provisions that afford them much more leeway in the firing process than that enjoyed by secular corporations. Even so, those processes must be followed, and clear communication to the staff person being terminated is a must, both for legal and for ethical reasons. Regardless of the employee's suitability for the position, that person is a child of God who is part of the church of Jesus Christ and should be treated as such. To do so provides the best possible example of the integrity to itself and to the world. Here are some key reminders for dealing with a termination of employment.

- Be clear about the reasons for termination. During, and especially after, termination, ensure that any official communication is accurate. Denominational officials and even attorneys may be needed to assist in these matters.
- If conflict is a factor in the termination, focus upon the actions and not the person. Clarify that the church's love of the person terminated is not in question but that his or her actions made the termination necessary.
- Follow agreed-upon local and denominational procedures. This not only protects the church from legal liability but also demonstrates that the church and its leaders are under authority and have credibility in dismissing an employee under its authority.
- Ensure that the dismissed employee is reasonably cared for. Where possible, favor compassion in regard to things like severance pay, the needs of the terminated employee's family, and seeing to the personal well-being of the terminated staff person. In this way, the church should differentiate itself from the sometimes cold environment of the corporate world. Sadly, the corporate world often does a better job of communicating up-front principles regarding hiring, firing, position descriptions, and legal boundaries than churches do. While we should create an atmosphere that takes seriously the church as a "family," we should not neglect sharing clearly the expectations of what it means to work in an accountable position in the church.

## DOING BUSINESS WITH CHURCH MEMBERS

Should the church engage in business relationships with members of the congregation? Whether or not it is advisable to enter into a business agreement with a church member depends upon several factors, the most important of which is conflict of interest. The ability to exercise proper pastoral care and oversight of certain ministries also come into play. For instance, would the business relationship compromise the minister's ability to exercise objective judgment about aspects of the parishioner's character or ministry, the church's budget, or accountability? If the business relationship would compromise the pastor's objectivity regarding the parishioner's role in the church, the business relationship is inadvisable. The same would apply to churches or boards in engaging the services of congregation members for things like insurance, construction, or catering. Would entering into a contract with the particular businessperson cloud the church board's approach to healthy stewardship? Is there pressure to avoid seeking competitive alternatives to the church member's business? If the answer to either question is yes, it is ethically advisable to avoid doing business with the church member.

In all church business, it is tempting to disregard the foundational identity of the church to produce short-term efficiency. However, the essential identity of the church, including its function as an example of the ways of Jesus Christ, should govern our decisions. This allows the church to do good business while also preserving its long-term witness.

## READY TO DO BUSINESS: A PREVENTATIVE MAINTENANCE CHECKLIST

The following checklist is meant to serve as a summary of up-front items to address when doing business in the church and community:

1. Reputation: *Have I entered into the type of agreement that would do no harm to the reputation of Christ if its details were made known?*

2. Conflict of Interest: *Are there any personal or professional conflicts of interest that would harm the mission or reputation of my ministry or of the church?*

3. Due Diligence: *Have I worked within the proper parameters and boundaries of the church, including pursuing a representative range of bidders/contractors and ensuring key decision-makers were consulted before entering into a business arrangement?*

4. Justice: *Is there anything in the business arrangement that would cast a shadow upon the church's view of social justice (e.g., unfair labor practices)?*

These four key guidelines, along with the detailed discussion in the chapter about the business of the church, can allow churches and even denominational entities to do the day-to-day business necessary for the mission of the church to go forth while also distinguishing the church as upholding exemplary standards of ethics and social justice.

## Mentoring Questions

1. Discuss your personal boundaries regarding doing business with members of the congregation you serve.

2. If you are bivocational, discuss the boundaries between your parishioners as those under your pastoral care and as potential customers or consumers. What up-front guidelines have you (or should you) set for yourself?

3. Evaluate the strength of your church's accountability process for handling monies and making business decisions. What, if anything, would you change?

4. How would you choose to deal with someone in the congregation who was doing business with the church or in the community in an unethical fashion?

## Suggested Reading

Batstone, David. *Saving the Corporate Soul—and (Who Knows?) Maybe Your Own.* New York: Jossey-Bass, 2003.

Christopher, J. Clif. *The Church Money Manual: Best Practices for Finance and Stewardship.* Nashville: Abingdon Press, 2014.

Hill, Alexander. *Just Business: Christian Ethics in the Marketplace.* Downers Grove, IL: InterVarsity Press, 2008.

Malphurs, Aubrey, and Steve Stroope. *Money Matters in Church: A Practical Guide for Leaders.* Grand Rapids: Baker Books, 2007.

# 8

## ETHICAL WORSHIP

## AND PREACHING

"Pastor, I am concerned about the worship group that leads us on second Sundays," the church member began. "They are loud, and many of us, especially in the earlier service, do not know the songs they are singing. It creates disruption in our worship experience!"

These words are all too familiar signs of the so-called worship wars that have dominated many conversations in church life in recent years. There are a myriad of books that address ways to implement change in the church. There are also a great number of books advocating ways to negotiate changes specifically in worship and preaching styles. The scope of this book does not include ways to address worship and preaching but rather the ethical dimensions of worship, including preaching and other liturgical elements.

There is an ancient Christian saying that states, in Latin, *Lex Orandi, Lex Credendi*, which means "The Law of Prayer, The Law of Belief." This is often translated "As we worship, so will we believe and live." For centuries, this phrase has reminded the church that what we do in worship shapes how we live out our theology. Worship and ethics are inseparably related. With this in mind, we will address the so-called worship wars while also examining ways in which our liturgy (the things we do in worship) and our approach to preaching flow from as well as inform our theology and ethics.

## THE CAUSE OF THE WAR

Frontier religion of the American West, along with the revivalist movements of the mid- to late-nineteenth century saw the rise of simplified worship structures, sometimes in reaction against what were perceived as cold, high church settings of worship and sometimes out of necessity. The simplification of the worship service itself is a trend that also dates back to the nineteenth century.[1] This simplified worship—focusing mainly on music, extemporaneous prayer, and preaching— became a staple of the revivalist movements of that period. Most denominations that emerged from or benefitted in some way from these movements maintained a relatively simple approach to worship, doing away with some ancient liturgical elements such as public reading of Scripture, responsive readings, corporate written prayers, and frequent celebration of Communion.[2] In the late 1970s, new approaches to church music emerged. The introduction of a more contemporary, popular style of music brought the inclusion of a wider variety of instruments, including guitars and drums. Given the elimination, or at least the sparse inclusion, of many other liturgical elements, music became the focal point of worship gatherings. Preaching, rather than Communion, continued to be highly valued and the climactic point of the worship service, but music and singing became the most participatory element.[3]

Music has always been a key element of Christian worship. The exclusion or limitation of the creeds, the Lord's Prayer, public reading of Scripture, responsive readings, and Communion in some segments of Christianity has narrowed even the definition of worship to mean the music performed during the service. With music being virtually the only highly participatory element in many worship gatherings, it is easy to see why changing musical styles and newer songs became a source of tension, leading to conflict in many churches. Recent trends in broadening the definition of worship to include more than music has assisted many congregations in moving beyond this conflict.[4]

Also, the use of tools such as the Revised Common Lectionary has assisted many of those responsible for planning worship, to work scriptural themes into all elements of the worship service. When exploring together the message of Scripture is the focus of a worship gathering, the elements of the service become means to an end, not an end in themselves. This moves the focus away from musical styles, allowing the congregation to embrace both ancient and modern worship tools without unnecessary focus on one particular element. Furthermore, it moves the congregation away from consumer-driven models of worship—which do not differentiate well between the kingdom of God and the kingdoms of the world—and enables the church to recapture its prophetic, countercultural voice. As Stanley Hauerwas and William Willimon note in their now classic work titled *Resident Aliens*, pastors must become more than simply "court chaplains, presiding over ceremonies of culture," or "court prostitutes" selling their love for the approval of upwardly mobile and bored people who, "more than anything else, want some relief from the anxiety brought on by their materialism."[5] Gathering to worship, then, becomes a time when we "retell and are held accountable to God's story, the adventure story about what God is doing with us in Christ."[6]

## RECAPTURING THE RHYTHM OF WORSHIP

Our culture is much more driven by Monday than by Sunday. There are even calendars that begin the week with Monday instead of Sunday. Monday represents the workweek, the nose-to-the-grindstone culture that drives us and, in many ways, defines us. Monday sets the tone for many of us. A *Family Circus* cartoon depicts a father with his briefcase heading out the door for another Monday with the caption, "Off to the rat race." The second caption depicts his son, holding a lunchbox and books, also heading out the door, with the caption, "Well, off to the mouse race."

Though Saturday (actually Friday evening through Saturday evening) was the Sabbath—the day of rest and of worshipful reflection—for the Jewish people, the New Testament records a key emphasis upon the "first day of the week" (Sunday): Jesus was raised from the dead on the first day of the week (Matt. 28:1-7), the Holy Spirit came at Pentecost on the first day of the week (Acts 2:1), and Paul instructed the church in Corinth to set aside funds "on the first day of every week" (1 Cor. 16:1-2). Though the disciples met together daily at first, eventually the first day of the week, the day of resurrection, became consistent as the time for Christians to gather for worship. The fellowship (Greek, *koinōnia*), worship, breaking of the bread, prayer, and compassion practiced corporately on this day of worship (see Acts 2:42) set the tone for the mission of the church throughout the week.

How can we recapture Sunday—our gathering for worship—as the day that sets the tone for our week? To do that, we will have to be more intentional in creating worship and preaching experiences that bear directly on how we live between Sundays.

Eugene Peterson states that worship is essentially a training ground for prayer. In many cultures, the question is not "Where do you worship?" but "Where do you pray?" If our worship gatherings are to be the hub in preparing us to live out the truths of the gospel, examining the content of our worship gatherings, then, is essential in preventative maintenance. We must allow the Holy Spirit to create an environment for worship that sets the tone for our service to Christ and others during the week.

We will examine some traditional elements of a worship service and briefly describe their ethical impact upon those who gather and participate. Many of these elements will be new or foreign to some Christians who have known only the simplified worship structures that have been the most popular for the last two hundred years or so. However, participatory worship is a concept that dates back to the oldest forms of worship in the Jewish tradition. These practices offer additional opportunities for lay involvement in worship beyond singing and giving. Singing and giving are important elements of worship, of course, but traditional worship activities increase participation and help parishioners internalize the worship experience so that it can be lived out in a consistent Christian ethic.

## Call to Worship

The call to worship is a proclamation that a sacred hour has arrived. A time has come for the people of God to gather in the name of Christ the risen Lord to offer sacrificial praises to God and to interact with God's Spirit through sacred fellowship with other believers. This is not simply a time to say "Good morning," since we can hear good morning in a local café. Rather, it is a time to evoke the reality of a special gathering: "We are called together in the name of the risen Christ to worship today." This is more than a difference in semantics. It is a way of setting the tone theologically and ethically to distinguish what is done in worship from other experiences throughout our week.

## Lighting of Candles

Candlelighting to denote a time of sacred assembly also has roots in the Jewish tradition, where candles are lit on Friday evening to represent the presence of God on the Sabbath. In Christian worship, even in more free, nonformal liturgical settings, candles represent the presence of Christ in our midst, evoking that reality Jesus taught us: "Where two or three gather in my name, there am I with them" (Matt. 18:20). Candles also have a traditional place in prayer, with the light of the candle shining throughout the service reminding us both of the ongoing intercession of the Spirit of God as we worship and of our own, continual prayer that is part of the walk with Christ (1 Thess. 5:17).

## Songs of Praise

The worship wars are really conflicts about music: its styles, tempo, words, and instrumentation. Like all other elements of liturgy, worship music is to be more than entertainment or a way of appeasing popular tastes. Music is a sacred gift that can move people toward a divine encounter. Even the harmony present in music is a reminder that although we do not all sing the same notes, we work together to help one another sing in the same key. Musician and theologian Jeremy Begbie suggests that the harmony of music best articulates both the separateness of God and others and the way those separate elements come together as one, "occupying the same space at the same time."[7]

Much has been written about changes in musical style and the oversimplification of lyrics in the repertoire of contemporary worship. Suffice it to say that our singing in worship is a form of prayer. What we pray will influence how we live. If our approach to music is consumer-driven (chosen because it appeals to *me*), that will shape our lives outside of Sunday. We are part of the most marketed-to generation in human history, having twenty-four-hour access to product appeals from all over the world. Breaking the stronghold of consumerism is a key to embracing the gospel of Jesus, which calls us to deny ourselves and sacrificially serve God and others. Creating a service that reflects both our debt to those gone before and our appreciation for what God is doing today gives a balanced picture of the fullness of the Christian life. To simply target a particular group through music brings an air of shallowness to the gospel. Furthermore, choosing songs of *any* era without considering the theological soundness of the words can lead to serious misunderstanding of what it means to know and serve God. Requiring a balance of styles and eras in worship music teaches harmony and unity, not just as musical concepts but as a lifestyle that crosses generational and cultural lines, just as the gospel intends.

## Public Reading of Scripture

It is surprising that the evangelical movement, which takes the Bible so seriously, includes so little Bible reading in worship services. We are quick to assert our love of the Bible and its message, but we often neglect the public reading of Scripture. We often read it before our sermons, of course. However, publicly reading the Bible in a thematic way from the various genres of Scripture demonstrates the "sacred thread" of God's love and salvation throughout this diverse book. Public reading also reminds us of our unity as, to paraphrase John Wesley, people of one book.

## Corporate Prayer

Praying together is a key reminder that we are a people who seek God together. Although individual prayers and devotions are important to our walk with Christ, our ultimate calling is to be a new kind of community. This is what John Wesley meant when he said that all holiness is "social holiness." The term *social holiness* can describe the work of God's people as change agents in our culture, but it also implies that the Christian life is meant to be lived in community. The most important thing the community can do is to consistently pray for God's leadership, provision, healing, and promotion of social change locally and globally. Intentionally setting aside time to participate in prayer together under the leadership of a designated prayer (usually the pastor) is a key act of worship that shapes who we are and how we live as a people.

## The Offering

Before the Eucharist was the primary focus of worship gatherings, and certainly before the sermon became the focus, the offering was the climactic element of the worship gatherings of the people of God. Sacrifices of praise—gifts given as sacrifices to God and to assist those in need—were a central part of worship in the Old Testament. In our contemporary, consumerist culture, which places such high value on gaining money and goods, the essential element of giving often gets swept aside. Indeed, the time of sacrificial giving in many congregations is surrounded not by prayer and encouragement but with apologies or with a kind of embarrassment at having to "pay the bills." The offering, however, is not simply to keep the church current on expenses. The true concept behind the offerings is that Christians are a giving community. Indeed, we believe that we are never so much like God as when we give: "For God so loved the world that he *gave* . . ." (John 3:16, emphasis added).

Giving in the way that the church has traditionally given is a radical act. There is a fun story about the little boy who, having come to church on the church bus, reported to his parents, who had stayed home, his favorite part of the experience. "Was it the music or the sermon?" his mother asked. "Those were okay, I guess," the boy replied, "but my favorite part was when they passed out that big plate full of money!"

Of course, we actually pass around an empty plate, and we fill the plate with money that we earned during the week as a way of recognizing that God is the provider of all things. None of us is self-made in regard to our success or our finances. We are recipients of God's gifts and blessings. We dedicate all that we have and all that we are for God's use. When we give, we are saying we trust that God can do more with the amount we have remaining than we could do on our own by keeping all of it! This is an ethical act: it is a way of imitating the God who gives by being people who give, expecting nothing in return for what we put in the plate. As we trust God with our resources, we become people whose lifestyles reflect both the giving spirit of Jesus and consistent trust in the God who provides. Therefore, relegating the offering to a kind of interruption or commercial break in the service denigrates an act that is tied to the earliest expressions of both Jewish and Christian worship. Furthermore, when we recognize giving as a participatory act in worship, just like singing, we strengthen the church's example of trust and generosity in a self-centered, materialistic world. The offering is not primarily a business transaction but a holy act of trust and worship by the people of God, given to further the purposes of God in the world.

## The Sermon

The sermon has often been wrongly characterized as a "give and take" proposition: the preacher gives, the congregation takes. However, even the sermon is participatory.

Sermons require a specific kind of participation: active listening. Active listening is a lost art in our fast-paced, high-tech culture. We are so busy and so bombarded by stimuli that we have learned to tune out whatever we do not wish to hear. The sermon is one of the few remaining forms of communication that requires active listening. The minister must actively listen to and share the key truths of the biblical text, and congregants must, in the words of one preacher, "lean forward" in order to apprehend the message and apply it to their own lives.

The preacher is charged to be true to the message of Scripture "in season and out of season" (2 Tim. 4:2), as most ordination vows remind us. The preacher cannot become the puppet of a particular group within the congregation, nor can he or she be a slave to the whims of a particular country or party. The sermon must be a transformational element. It is the moment when those actively listening really hear from God concerning the world around them, the kingdom of God that has come, and their own ethical choices throughout the week.

The use of audiovisual materials can enhance the effectiveness of the message, but these are no substitute for the countercultural art of active listening. Jesus's communication techniques consisted of parables, metaphors, and other examples set before the people to help them grasp the message of a radical new kingdom. In our overly saturated audiovisual culture, it is countercultural, almost unique, to stand before a congregation to convey a message to our fellow believers in a way that invites them to an encounter with the living God. While God uses the personality of the preacher to convey the message, the preacher should not be the driving force. Nor should raw emotion, although emotions are also important tools to get God's message across. Neither personality nor emotion (including emotions drummed up by technology) should substitute for prayerful preparation both of the message and of the messenger. The deliverer and the hearers of the sermon both practice an important skill: humble, active listening. This kind of participation, along with the words of the message itself, helps us become the humble, attentive, and compassionate disciples we are called to be.

As an act of worship, preaching is a reminder that all who participate in worship are under the authority of God as revealed in Jesus Christ through Scripture. The preacher recognizes his or her role as spokesperson for the ways of God, and therefore listens, prays, and prepares accordingly. Those who actively listen to the sermon recognize that they are not simply hearing a preacher but they are seeking to hear the very message of God delivered through the craft of preaching.

## The Lord's Supper

John Wesley advised his ministers to partake at the table of the Lord as often as possible. For centuries, this simple participatory meal, which was called the Eucharist, from the Greek word *eucharisto*, meaning thanksgiving, was the focal point of Christian worship gatherings.[8] The Reformation brought a renewed focus upon preaching, given the rise in literacy and, with the invention of the printing press, the prominence of the written word over symbols. However, downplaying the use of material elements in worship, such as the bread and the cup in the Lord's Supper, risks the loss of key theological and ethical symbols. As theologian Rob Staples notes, the basic insight gleaned from participation in the Eucharist is that "God can work the spiritual through the material."[9] The Eucharist is an important focal point in Christian worship because it reminds us that, among other things, matter is not necessarily evil but can be "a carrier of divine grace."[10]

As most ministers know, there is a wide range of beliefs attached to the eucharistic meal. For some, it is a *sacred memorial*, commemorating the sacrificial death of Jesus on the cross. For others (including those in the Roman Catholic, Lutheran,

Orthodox, and Wesleyan traditions), the Eucharist brings the actual presence of Jesus Christ, and his grace is attached to this meal in a special or unusual way.[11] Regardless of the specific significance the community attaches to the Communion meal, a few key theological and ethical considerations are in order.

- **Unity**. Communion allows the entire community of faith, regardless of economic, ethnic, or racial background, to find common ground at the table of Christ, reminding us all of the unity in love that the person and work of Jesus Christ provide.

- **Hope**. Communion is a recognition not only of the sacrificial love of God displayed through Jesus Christ but also of the hope-filled anticipation that all believers share in the return of Jesus Christ to set all things right and to make all things new.

- **Openness**. Communion provides a direct encounter in a tactile, participatory way with the grace of God: we are obeying Jesus's direct command to his disciples by partaking of this meal, and, therefore, we welcome the maturing of our faith.

- **Mission**. Finally, this participation causes us to be "breathed out," in Brent Peterson's words, in unity under the umbrella of the mission of Christ, even though we are departing to go our separate ways.[12] The bread and the cup strengthen Christians for the work of the kingdom of God.

Although there is a trend among evangelicals toward increasing the frequency of participation in the Eucharist, ministers frequently hear or share of fears about making the sacred commonplace or overly ritualized by repeating it too frequently. However, all elements of the worship service can become commonplace if not done intentionally. This does not stop us from singing songs every week, preaching sermons every week, or sending around the offering plate every week!

Each of these acts, along with Communion, are instruments God uses to transform us, which is John Wesley's definition of a "means of grace."

Since Jesus's own introduction of Communion to his disciples, the Eucharist has been the focal point of nearly all Christian worship traditions. We are eucharistic people in every sense of the term: we are thankful people who experience God's grace, we are a gathered people who reverence God's presence in our midst, and we are humble people who honor the image of God in all people regardless of racial or economic differences. We are a sent people: a people sent together under the banner of the love of Jesus Christ to be (corporately) the presence of Christ and his ways in the world. Therefore, frequent participation in this act of worship should be, as Wesley recommended, of utmost importance. This act, more than any other, defines the ethical character of the church of Jesus Christ.

## The Altar Call

According to some, evangelical Protestant tradition has elevated the altar call, a response to the sermon in which people are invited to gather around an altar of prayer, above Communion as the focal point of the worship experience. For many, a sermon without a public altar call is somehow incomplete. Yet others see the sermon as preparation for the eucharistic meal; they point to the idea that we gather together around both "Word and Table."[13] Participation in the Lord's Supper is indeed a public response to the sermon, as is the altar call in its varying forms. It is noteworthy that Jesus called his disciples and others to make public commitments. This aids in establishing the ethical place of the public altar call in worship.

The journey of Jesus's followers began with public and intentional commitments to follow Christ, from the calling of the Twelve to the very public responses at Pentecost. Since the early nineteenth century, the public response at an altar or "mourner's bench" has been a key component of American Christianity. However, some ethical boundaries regarding the use of an altar call are in order. The minister must avoid manipulative or shaming language that may cause congregants to respond to momentary feelings of guilt rather than a desire for a true life-changing encounter with Christ. Many of us remember the altar calls given at camp meetings each summer, many of which produced little more than emotional catharsis. Preachers should also note the kind of response the preaching text calls for. The responses we call for should connect to the text. Certainly, the Holy Spirit is free to evoke any number of responses, but we must be Spirit-led in our exegesis and use of the texts we are preaching.

Evangelist and sociologist Tony Campolo once remarked that his "dream altar call" would be for congregants to stand and, rather than coming forward, to exit.[14] Citing the late social activist Will D. Campbell, Campolo stated that this call would not be to "come forward" but "go to Jesus!"[15] Campolo imagined that this call might result in hospital administrators, nursing home directors, and even prison wardens reporting that congregation members were invading their places insisting that "Jesus is here" and that "they must see him!"[16] Perhaps the best measure of an altar call is the degree to which it draws to a culmination all elements of participatory worship, not just the sermon, with action by the hearers.

## Benediction

The term *benediction* literally means "a good word," or, more specifically, "a word of blessing." Brent Peterson reminds us that the benediction, the pronouncement of a blessing to the departing people of God, is a "hopeful charge, calling, and blessing" by which the people of the ministry of God are "exhaled by and with the Spirit" into the world.[17] The service begins with a blessing (call to worship) that, in a sense, covers the whole service. The benediction is meant to, in the words of late Reformed theologian Gilbert VanDooren, "cover our whole lives until the next Lord's Day."[18] The benediction is a word from God passed along by one who has been granted authority to remind those who have just participated in worship and heard the proclaimed Word. It is a reminder that they are under the watchful eye of God himself and are called to live together under the blessing and admonition of God, even as they depart from the sacred gathering.[19] Just as the call to worship is the starting gun for gathering the people of God to the specific event of corporate worship, the benediction sends them out together to their separate places of service. The benediction is a reminder to live out the words they have sung and heard, and to live in the eucharistic spirit in which they have just participated.

## Weddings and Funerals

One of my early mentors began a conversation by saying, "I don't do weddings." I was shocked. I even reminded him that I had attended a wedding he had performed! He clarified by saying, "What I mean is that my job description as a minister does not specify that I do weddings. The law and the church *allow* me to do weddings. What I do is oversee worship services in the church. That is my primary responsibility. So, if couples simply want to 'get hitched,' I send them to a judge or a justice of the peace. If they want to solemnize their vows in the context of worship in the church, then I may choose to officiate the wedding."

I have passed along my mentor's initial phrase to virtually every couple with whom I have participated in premarital counseling. After I give them a moment to look at each other in startled surprise, I explain the rest. This sets the tone for both how we prepare for and how they embrace the vow they will make to God, to each other, and to God's people in regard to fidelity and commitment. I must quickly add that, given the fact that the role of the minister is to instruct in matters of faith and practice in the church and that Christian weddings are "church weddings" regardless of whether they are performed in a church building, clergypersons must insist upon adequate time of preparation for couples.

There is now a myriad of materials available to assist ministers in doing preventative maintenance for marriage. When ministers don't require premarital counseling with the reasoning, "They will get married anyway, so why not do it in a church setting," they disregard the fact that marriage is not simply a contract between two parties but is a covenant between two parties and God in the presence of the people of God *as an act of worship.* In short, it is ethically questionable at best to perform a wedding without premarital preparation, given the fact that couples who have premarital counseling are far less likely to get divorced than those who do not. It is better to turn down the couple's request as a matter of principle and a matter of witness to the church's high view of marriage than to compromise in this area of premarital preparation.

Tom Long rightly bemoans the fact that the Christian funeral has become a bit of a relic in our death-denying culture. Long notes that, although many updated liturgies for Christian funerals have been developed over the last several decades, "American Christians, along with the rest of American culture, have become increasingly confused and conflicted about healthy ways to commemorate death."[20] Long sees this upheaval in ways we approach death as ethically important for the church: "The stakes are high. I am persuaded that in this, our moment in history, we are going through one of those periodic upheavals in the ways we care (or don't) for the dead that are inevitable signs of an upheaval in how we care (or don't) for the living."[21] Long adds that "a society that has forgotten how to honor the bodies of those who have departed is more inclined to neglect, even torture, the bodies of those still living."[22]

In order for a funeral to be a truly Christian funeral, historical theology and Christian ethics suggests the following important boundaries:

- The funeral must focus upon the worship of God, the giver of life and sustainer through death.
- The funeral must include an invitation to grieve as hope-filled grievers (see 1 Thess. 4:13).
- The funeral must portray the bigger story of God's redemption and grace rather than the story of the deceased. The deceased's story can be shared and celebrated as a part of the bigger story of God's love and mercy.
- Music, Scripture, and messages must point to the hope of all who are in Christ while acknowledging the impact of death upon those who remain.
- There must be clarity regarding the doctrine of the "resurrection of the body" (see 1 Cor. 15, the Apostles' Creed, the Nicene Creed, etc.). We do not eternally escape the body. Rather, our bodies shall be "raised imperishable" (1 Cor. 15:52-53). To avoid the doctrine of bodily resurrection downplays the importance the Bible places upon bodily existence.
- Death must be portrayed accurately, as normal, natural, and tragic. For the Christian, death is not the end of the story. Yet to deny the reality and pain of death downplays the power of true resurrection: that which is not truly dead cannot truly be raised.
- The funeral must teach a lesson about life: we will all die, and we will all live until we die. This means that we will one day be remembered for how our lives were lived. The body in the casket reminds us of both of

these realities, which call us to accountability for the choices we make with the time we have.

In remaking the funeral as something more than a pep rally or a kind of celebrity roast, we invoke both the finite nature of our time to live for Christ and the dramatic hope of the resurrection, which we have through Jesus, the one who has defeated death.

## ETHICAL PREACHING

The integrity and even goodness of a sermon have much to do with the credibility of the preacher. Many of us have experienced situations in which preachers who were not strong communicators were lauded by their congregation for their character and the care they provided to the people. Likewise, strong communicators and their sermons can be dismissed or even derided by congregants who perceive the speaker to be a "good preacher but not a good pastor." The character of the minister can cover a multitude of sins in regard to preaching style. Many of us who preach consistently are thankful for times when congregations responded positively to a poorly preached sermon because of their respect for the relationship we have with them.

This is not an excuse for failure to adequately prepare for and consistently grow in our work as preachers. For most of us who are ordained, the words of ordination spoken over us began with the biblical admonition of Paul to the young pastor named Timothy:

Preach the word; be prepared in season and out of season; correct, rebuke and encourage—with great patience and careful instruction. For the time will come when people will not put up with sound doctrine. Instead, to suit their own desires, they will gather around them a great number of teachers to say what their itching ears want to hear. They will turn their ears away from the truth and turn aside to myths. But you, keep your head in all situations, endure hardship, do the work of an evangelist, discharge all the duties of your ministry. (2 Tim. 4:2-5, emphasis added)

As preachers, our Christ-centered communication brings clarity to a world that is easily pulled away from the way of Christ. Preaching is not the only work we do as we "discharge all the duties of [our] ministry," but it is a chosen vehicle through which the message of Christ and Christ's ways are conveyed. The way in which we discharge our duties affects the perceived integrity of the message we preach. The converse is also true: the integrity of our preaching either sheds light or casts shadows on the rest of our work.

A closer look at the ethics of the preacher and of preaching is warranted, since so much of contemporary worship either flows toward or from the preaching moment. The Eucharist historically was the focal point of worship until it was displaced by the sermon during the Protestant Reformation. However, even in Communion-centered worship gatherings, the act of preaching takes up a good deal of the minister's time and attention.

## The Character of the Preacher

The missionary who shares stories that bring us to tears and motivate us to see the global perspective of the kingdom of God can quickly damage the message by sharing a story that is inaccurate or untrue. The pastor seeking to build credibility with his or her new congregation can become suspect if he or she claims a story as his or her own that belongs to someone else. Likewise, using personal grudges or difficult people in church as "sermon fodder" can turn the preacher into a bully in the eyes of the congregation.

One element of a Preaching Covenant (see Appendix A for a sample) should include this agreement by the minister: I will not preach *at* you. This means that we preachers agree not to utilize confidential information to single out people or problems in a sermon, and we will refrain from conveying a message to an individual via the corporate communication of the sermon. Instead, we choose to leave the work of convicting hearts to the Holy Spirit.

### Avoiding Manipulation

People will surely leave a service convicted of sin and moved toward a commitment to confessing their own sins after hearing certain sermons. However, this conviction should not result from singling people out in a passive-aggressive manner, dealing publicly with something that should have been addressed privately. As tempting as it may be to target a disgruntled or difficult parishioner from the "high ground" of the pulpit, this will only harm the reputation of the preacher and diminish the authority of the pulpit. In fact, the nature of preaching as proclamation of the message of God calls the preacher to preach *with* and *to* the congregation, and not *at* them. Preaching at the congregation in a manipulative or dictatorial manner places the preacher in the category of those to whom Jesus directed his sharpest rebuke: "blind guides" who, in their hypocrisy, "strain out a gnat but swallow a camel" (Matt. 23:24).

The preventative measures preachers can take in order to avoid these and other ethical errors in preaching begin with embracing the theological reality that preaching is, in the words of William Willimon, "peculiar speech."[23] The text of Scripture from which we draw our sermons is not simply a tool for making Christianity palatable to the world or even to church members. Rather, the interest of Scripture is "to create and to critique a new people."[24] We as preachers submit ourselves to the authority of the canonical texts and then pass along from that authoritative Word messages of the ways of God expressed through the person and work of Jesus Christ.

This is one reason preachers are more commonly turning to the Revised Common Lectionary for guidance in sermon and worship service preparation. As Justo and Catherine Gonzalez remind us: "Lectionaries are a very useful aid for preaching, for they prevent the preacher from centering on a few favorite passages, books, or themes."[25] Lectionary preaching takes away the temptation to simply preach at an issue or to pick out comfortable texts (i.e., those familiar to the preacher and to the congregation). The lectionary reminds us that we are always under assignment; we are told what to say by the authority of the church of Jesus Christ and Scripture. Like our listeners, we become attentive to the Spirit's movement through the body of Christ as expressed in the assigned texts. On a practical level, lectionary preachers cannot be easily accused of "preaching at" a person or an issue in the church. We can, in the words of Walter Brueggemann, "get down and hide behind the text," reminding the congregation that we, like they, are people in submission to the authority of the church and its book.[26]

## Avoiding Two Types of Political Correctness

Use of the lectionary is not the only way preachers can guard against misusing or misrepresenting Scripture in their preaching. Paul's warnings to Timothy include warnings against preaching what is popular to one's hearers. This does not mean avoiding so-called political correctness, however. It is, instead, recognizing that all groups and individuals along the political spectrum have their own version of political correctness. For instance, a preacher in a more conservative congregation can easily get "Amens" and other forms of affirmation by preaching about conservative social issues, thereby turning the pulpit into an extension of the hottest talk radio program. If we simply speak agreeably to a congregation about an issue on which we all agree, are we not practicing political correctness, whether the issue is on the "right" leaning or the "left"?

It is one thing to preach about the ills of, say, homosexual behavior. It is yet another to challenge a congregation to love those who are struggling with sexual identity or who feel that they are indeed homosexual. It is a kind of unhealthy accommodation to simply tickle the ears of congregants by opposing an issue that one's denomination or congregation opposes. It is more Christlike to challenge hearers to love one another as Christ has loved us, even if their lifestyles or actions differ from the theological and ethical standards set by Scripture and the church. One does not have to affirm a person's behavior in order to love as Christ loves, as Christ himself demonstrated throughout his ministry.

In the same way, progressive or liberal political correctness that seeks inclusion without transformation diminishes the impact of the peculiar speech to which we are called. The preaching of the gospel never causes us to rest easy as we are. The gospel invites us to come as we are and to love people as they are; yet, it expresses the kind of love that cares for us too much to keep us as we are.

Paul's admonition on "speaking the truth in love" (Eph. 4:15) includes two elements: truth and love. Truth is incomplete without love. Likewise, what we consider to be loving is incomplete if it is misleading in regard to the need for honest evaluation and transformation, both individually and corporately. Theological integrity in our submission to the text as those being transformed, resisting the temptation to use the text as a manipulative tool, and prayerful preparation that asks God to speak specifically through the message, are helpful markers of ethical preaching.

# PATRIOTIC AND SECULAR INFLUENCES ON WORSHIP

The focus of worship and preaching is Jesus Christ: his ways and his kingdom. This seems logical, since the church was created by Jesus to further the mission of God in the world. However, there are a few Sundays in a typical year when we ministers are tempted to turn the focus away from God and toward other things. Specifically, there are national and secular holidays that fall on or around particular Sundays of the year. It has become typical for churches and ministers to have "special services" around patriotic holidays or other secular events.

When we focus on the centrality of Jesus and following the ways of Jesus in our worship, we will move away from lesser goals—no matter how noteworthy they appear—that may shift our focus from the essential work of preparing each other to worship and serve God. However, in virtually every culture patriotic nostalgia has become an idol that tempts us to use one of our comparatively few opportunities to gather together for Christian worship to elevate a political or nationalistic agenda.

Once when visiting Russia, I remarked to our Russian guide—a minister and historian—that I was surprised that images of Russia's tsars from ages past were portrayed in stained glass in some historic churches. "Don't tell me an American is critical of patriotism in worship," she remarked with a smile. Her point was well taken. Apparently, Americans are well known for allowing patriotic fervor to outweigh zeal for worshiping God. We couch these sentiments in religious language at times. However, there is a marked difference in many services of worship on patriotic holidays. As one colleague remarked, "You can tell a difference between my congregation's response to a patriotic song and a worship song. The patriotic song evokes more tears, cheers, and praise!" This mingling of worship and patriotism borders on a kind of idolatry in many congregations; and idolatry, along with hypocrisy, is the sin most consistently opposed by God throughout the entirety of Scripture.

Here are questions to aid in maintaining healthy ethical boundaries in worship gatherings and in avoiding idolatry. Ask these questions when planning a worship order:

1. Do the songs chosen elevate Jesus Christ, or do they elevate a particular country or political agenda?
2. Given that the church is worldwide and universal, would someone from a nation different from the congregation's own feel disconnected from worship due to its patriotic nature?
3. Could an outside observer—either a nonchurched person or a person from another culture—distinguish between giving thanks for a nation and exalting a nation to a place that should be reserved for Christ?
4. Does the worship service, which is supposed to focus upon the Prince of Peace, exalt violence and war?
5. If the service honors those who have served or died in military service, does it do so without compromising the ultimate message of peace that Jesus exemplifies?
6. Is the sermon a history lesson, a political speech, or a kind of eulogy for the deceased devoid of the authority of Scripture and not focused on Christ?

We are citizens of an earthly nation, but also of a different kingdom. We can indeed be thankful for the nations into which we are born and in which we reside. However, these kingdoms, like all other kingdoms before and after, shall "become the kingdom of our Lord and of his Messiah" (Rev. 11:15). When we elevate any other kingdom by singing its praises in our worship or by telling its story instead of the story of God, we risk idolatry. This idolatry gives false hope to those who desperately need the hope found only in Christ. We really do live how we pray, and our worship and preaching set the boundaries of our lives as those who are to be in the world but not of it (see John 17:16). This distinction is seen most clearly when we are gathered together, being prepared to go into a lost and dying world that longs for a kingdom that will never end.

## Mentoring Questions

1. How do the current elements of your existing worship service influence how you and others in your congregation live? What liturgical elements would you add (or remove) from your service to more clearly emphasize the ethical nature of worship?

2. In what ways might your preaching be improved by applying the ethical guidelines discussed in this chapter?

3. How could you communicate your up-front boundaries about worship planning in regard to patriotic and secular holidays?

4. In what ways do the ethical boundaries discussed in this chapter help you envision the church as universal—that is, not bound or controlled by a particular culture?

## Suggested Reading

Dawn, Marva. *Reaching Out Without Dumbing Down: A Theology of Worship for This Urgent Time.* Grand Rapids: Eerdmans, 1995.

Long, Thomas G. *The Witness of Preaching.* Louisville, KY: Westminster John Knox Press, 2005.

Peterson, Brent. *Created to Worship: God's Invitation to Become Fully Human.* Kansas City: Beacon Hill Press of Kansas City, 2012.

Salter, Darius. *Preaching as Art.* Kansas City: Beacon Hill Press of Kansas City, 2008.

Staples, Rob. *Outward Sign, Inward Grace: The Place of Sacraments in Wesleyan Spirituality.* Kansas City: Beacon Hill Press of Kansas City, 1991.

Webber, Robert E. *Ancient-Future Church.* Grand Rapids: Baker Books, 2008.

Willimon, William H. *Peculiar Speech: Preaching to the Baptized.* Grand Rapids: Eerdmans, 1992.

# 9

# FAILING, FALLING, AND
# THE ETHICS OF GRACE

In his classic work *The Grace Awakening*, pastor and author Charles Swindoll presents two scenarios regarding failure, using the analogy of parents instructing a teenager who has just received a driver's license. There are two instructions a parent could give, according to Swindoll. A parent might choose to say something like this: "Now let me remind you, you're going to have a wreck. So the first thing you need to do is to memorize the number of our insurance agent. That way, when you have an accident, you can be sure to call the right number. But here are the keys. Hope you enjoy the drive." Or, a parent might say something like this to a new driver in the family: "You have had excellent training, and you have keys. Sometimes accidents happen, and when they do, here is how to handle them. However, accidents aren't normal; they're the exception. You are trained to drive, so enjoy the drive."[1] One speech illustrates a fear-based approach, and the other a grace-centered approach. Every church chooses one of those two approaches to dealing with failure among its members— fear based or grace centered.

Pastoral leaders are responsible to set the proper tone in a local church. Will it be a place of fear or of expectation? Will leaders develop cynicism toward themselves and others, or will they establish an environment of hope and trust? Too often, healthy risk taking in mission-centered ministry is interrupted by fear and cynicism. Yet given time and intentionality, the atmosphere that the pastor and others choose to promote will prevail. Failure does not have to be fatal.

We will address two kinds of failure in this chapter: missional failure and moral failure. Neither need be fatal to the ministry of the pastor or of the congregation. The key to recovery lies in the kind of environment churches and church leaders choose to promote.

## THE ETHICS OF MISSIONAL FAILURE

"This will hurt you politically," said one district leader in response to a young pastor's plan to implement needed change in her congregation. She walked away discouraged and less willing to risk beginning a new ministry that might help the congregation become more relevant and vibrant within its changing community. Another denominational leader, after receiving the résumé of a recently ousted pastor, simply cast it aside, stating, "I don't want a troublemaker on this district so close to my retirement." The leader had little interest in looking more deeply at the pastor's context, which involved taking a firm stand against past emotional abuses by the congregation he had served.

Neither of these leaders was guided by a proper ethic of failure. When Christian leaders create an environment in

which people are allowed to fail while attempting theologically and ethically sound ventures, we cast a vision for long-term
growth and creativity that flows directly from the creative and
forgiving God we serve. When leaders squelch risk taking,
they risk squelching obedience to Jesus, who time and again
called his followers to take risks. A key element of preventative
maintenance is to be honest about risks. It is true that they do
not always produce the results we hope for. However, calculated, Spirit-led risks can result in long-term church health
and a stronger witness in the community. Allowing leaders at
local and denominational levels to risk short-term losses for
long-term, Christ-centered goals is a key element of ethical
Christian leadership.

In his book *The Other Side of Pastoral Ministry*, Daniel
Brown notes that risk avoidance is among the strongest elements in church life that prevent meaningful change. Brown
states, "Serving Christ requires one risk after another. . . . Risk
is dangerous and potentially painful. But if we don't step out
of the boat as Peter did on the Sea of Galilee, we accomplish
little for Christ."[2]

Unfortunately, an emphasis upon short-term gains in
attendance and giving has diverted many church and denominational leaders from the overall goal of making Christlike disciples. This has led many churches and church leaders toward
either a fear-based approach to ministry or one that shies away
from taking calculated, Spirit-led risks to further the mission of
Christ. Both of these approaches, as Jones and Armstrong remind, keep pastoral ministry from becoming what it is intended
to be: a "'still more excellent way' of love that leads toward the
*telos*, the goal, of God's reign in its fullness."[3]

For this "more excellent way" of Christian ministry to
prevail, church leaders, both locally and denominationally,
must reacquaint themselves with the ethics of failure. In short,
the ethics of failure involve the willingness to risk apparent

short-term failure for long-term health. Jesus, at the time of his death, was viewed, even by his closest followers, as a kind of failure. Jesus risked losing his very life, time and again turning down opportunities for short-term recognition. The Bible describes this choice in the following way: "For the joy set before him [Jesus] endured the cross, scorning its shame, and sat down at the right hand of the throne of God" (Heb. 12:2). The joy that transcended the apparent failure of the cross was the long-term gain of being at the Father's right hand. Too often, ministers are discouraged from asserting sound theological or ethical principles in fear of appearing as a failure in the eyes of their own leaders, who are judging by less-than-biblical standards of success.

When leaders create a standard of goodness that reflects secular, not kingdom, values, church health wanes and long-term callousness toward the ways of God increases. The solution is to create up-front agreements that encourage risk taking to achieve Christ-centered goals. Even what Brown calls "bloopers"—mistakes made with good, Christ-centered, missional intent—will be opportunities for growth and education, strengthening the church and its leaders for future endeavors. According to Brown, mistakes should be viewed as lessons and can bring about "an atmosphere of warmth and love in the church" that draws people together.[4] A church that creates an up-front ethic of failure could include the following statements:

- Our priorities will reflect the mission of God rooted in sound theology. (See the Grid for Ethical Decision-Making in Appendix A.)
- Our decisions will be well-communicated and will be bathed in prayer.
- Our ventures will be in harmony with the mission of this church and with one another.
- Our failures will be sources of growth and not sources of shame.

- Our successes will be building blocks for taking future, calculated, Spirit-led risks to continue the work of God's mission through us.
- Our failures and successes will teach us how to live together as God's community more effectively.
- Our failures and successes will neither discourage us nor define us: Our identity is rooted in the person and work of Jesus Christ, who seeks to accomplish his will through us.

Creating a statement of this kind will redefine success for a church and its leaders. This new, Christ-centered definition of success will replace the fear of failure and encourage godly risk taking, helping to create an environment of long-term, Spirit-led church health and multiplication. This is in line with the theological and ethical goals of the Christ who calls his people to launch out into the deep (cf. Luke 5:4) and follow his ways.

To practice a healthy ethic of failing requires evaluating the definition and causes of the failure, forgiving where necessary, implementing corrective actions, and moving again toward worthwhile goals. Pastors who create an environment in which risks can be taken often foster an environment where failure is seen as necessary at times in order to find the ministry approach that best fits God's vision for the church. Those who fear risk or who shame those who venture and fail perpetuate the status quo, or, even worse, contribute to the decline of theological and ethical standards. This eventually kills the prophetic witness of the church. Leaders at every level of church life who fear the political fallout of opposing those whose values do not align with the kingdom of God only exacerbate the problem and bear great responsibility for the ultimate failure of a church or a denomination—even while they may celebrate counterfeit, short-term success.

# THE ETHICS OF MORAL FAILURE

Moral failure occurs when the ways of Christ are cast aside, the importance of the community of faith is abandoned, and the goals of Christ are replaced with selfish goals. The term *moral failure* describes a variety of acts so serious in nature that they jeopardize the position and even the ordination credentials of a minister. One of the purposes of this book is to help avoid, or at least prepare to deal with, the moral and ethical problems that can hinder the effectiveness of the minister. Healthy boundaries for ethical Christian ministry include a strong grounding in the ways of Jesus, a high view of one's place as part of the community of faith, willingness to sacrifice short-term gain or pleasure for long-term results, and a recognition that each of us is called to be shaped and molded into the image of Christ.[5] (Refer to the Grid for Ethical Decision-Making in Appendix A.) Moral failure occurs when one or more of these elements are neglected. We will examine this neglect and the moral failure that follows in two categories: doctrine and relationships.

## Doctrinal Failure

When we leave the ways of Jesus, we succumb to doctrinal error. This is indeed a kind of moral failure since the church is a theological entity by definition: the church is created by Jesus to be the centerpiece for instruction regarding God and God's ways. Therefore, straying doctrinally is a failure to teach and preach in a manner consistent with orthodox Christian teaching. The remedy for doctrinal failure is the corrective voice of leaders—both contemporary leaders and those from history—who are used by the Holy Spirit to establish doctrinal boundaries for the church. Old and New Testament corrective texts address both doctrinal and relational errors. In recent decades, the de-emphasis of sound doctrinal training in favor of more pragmatic or practical training has created a situation in which relational issues now account for much of the church's corrective work. It could also be that our failure to address the church's doctrinal and missional identity, including emphasizing a wrong identity for the church, has contributed to the rise in relational failures.

## Relational Failure

In the classic play *The Crucible* by Arthur Miller, John, a main character whose family is being suspected of witchcraft during the Salem witch hysteria of the late 1600s, is asked by the local minister to recite the Ten Commandments as a test of his faithfulness to God. Nervously, John begins his recitation and after two attempts keeps coming up with only nine. Exasperated, he looks toward his wife for help: "Adultery, John. You forgot adultery." This is a telling scene, since only John and his wife know that he himself had committed the sin of adultery with a woman in the village. This reminds us how easy it is to forget or overlook our own relationship failures. The sins of others are easier to track than our own.

According to writer and counselor J. Keith Miller, this is because at its deepest level, sin is "putting ourselves in the center of our lives and [at the center of] other people's lives where only God should be."[6] Moral failures in ministry often occur when, out of either selfish ambition or desperate isolation, we substitute ourselves for something that only God can supply. As a mentor of mine once said, "We are all grace receivers; none of us is the source of grace." While space here does not allow for a full examination of the moral temptations found in Christian ministry, the following diagnostic questions provide a start on preventative maintenance against moral failure in relationships.

*1. What is the state of my relationship priorities?* Am I maintaining healthy communication and appropriate intimacy with my spouse? Do I have an outlet for energy and attention that is not work related? Am I maintaining my personal physical and spiritual health, aside from the work I do in preparation for ministering and counseling?

2. *Am I saying no consistently?* Are there things on my calendar that should be delegated? Am I being proactive or reactive in regard to my time?

3. *Am I showing signs of codependency?* Codependence occurs when a person centers his or her life around managing the behavior of another, usually due to fear of confrontation. This obsession can manifest itself in a desire to control the other person, a desperate need for approval, or a consistent attraction to unhealthy relationships.[7]

4. *Does anyone else know what I am doing on the Internet?* Sharing passwords with a spouse or a trusted friend, giving access to our search engines to another person, and even implementing accountability software at home and in the office can keep us from drifting toward unhealthy online distractions.

5. *Am I relying on unhealthy or addictive behaviors or substances to relieve stress?* Sit down with a mentor, a spouse, or trusted friend and evaluate how you relieve stress. Stress is real, and it has to have a release point. Too often, unhealthy stress relievers such as emotional or physical affairs, drug or alcohol abuse, or pornography are substituted for healthy ways of receiving affirmation or of relieving stress.

6. *Are my finances in order?* Unethical financial dealings are a betrayal of key relationships. Therefore, the minister should make sure his or her financial dealings reflect integrity and transparency in relationship to the minister's home, the community, and the church.

7. *Is there unconfessed sin in my life?* Small areas of disobedience can snowball into bigger issues. Finding someone to whom we can "confess [our] sins" so that we "may be healed" is crucial in keeping our conscience clean and our future interactions ethical (see James 5:16).

## Remedies for Moral Failure

Scriptural models for addressing sin in the church, particularly that found in Matthew 18:15-20, underlie the Communication Covenant presented in this book and have guided the approach of the church in dealing with sin throughout its history. This model involves one-to-one confrontation followed by the involvement of a few key others and then, when needed, sharing the matter with the entire congregation. The purpose of this process is to restore, not shame, the offender. The ideal expressed in Scripture begins with confession and moves toward full restoration: "whoever turns a sinner from the error of their way will save them from death and cover over a multitude of sins" (James 5:20). This implies that moral failures should be neither overlooked nor treated as unpardonable. When restoring one who has failed morally, the Bible and Christian experience demonstrate three key principles to keep in mind.

First, some sins can be overcome only through ongoing accountability. Twelve-step programs have demonstrated that sins involving addictive behavior are best addressed in community. During his ministry, Jesus warned his disciples that there are some things that can be overcome only "by prayer and fasting" (Mark 9:29, KJV). Likewise, certain behaviors—including sexual addiction and drug addiction—can be overcome only by consistent interaction in a trusted group or one-on-one setting.

Second, though we may have been fully forgiven and restored by God, a process of discipline may yet have to take place. Christians, especially Christians in church leadership, are representatives of the church universal. When we experience moral failure, those in authority over us may deem it necessary to publicly admonish us even by removing us from ministry responsibilities for a period of time—sometimes permanently. This does not mean that we are not or cannot be forgiven. Nor is this discipline necessarily mean-spirited. As people under authority, it is incumbent upon ministers and other leaders who have experienced serious moral failure to participate in the up-front disciplinary process of their church in order to demonstrate true repentance, experience personal restoration, and restore the trust that has been broken. This is a necessary and, ultimately, a healing process.

Third, the severity of the impact of a moral failure generally determines the scope of its consequences. For example, those who have been entrusted with greater responsibilities should expect that their moral failure will be treated more publicly and with more severity than the failure of those with lesser responsibilities. All sin may be equally bad in the sight of God, but the consequences and impact of sins upon the church differ based upon the perpetrator, the number of victims, and the overall nature of the infraction.

As long as the goals of the local church or denomination are ultimately redemptive to the good name of Christ, to his church, to the victim, and to the individual who has fallen, then a healthy foundation exists for confession, accountability, and the restorative work of the Holy Spirit to be realized through the church. My own denomination provides an example of this concerning the issue of divorce. Those who have been divorced and who apply for their first level of ministerial licensure are asked to submit to a rather extensive review of the situations surrounding the divorce: letters from witnesses, testimonies of the nature of the divorce, testimonies even of the divorced spouse when possible, and so on. Candidates submit to this process knowing that there is no guarantee that denominational officials will approve their request to remove the barrier of divorce from their pursuit of full ordination. When the process is complete, the records have been reviewed, and interviews have been conducted with the candidate, the candidate may indeed be cleared to move forward in the lengthy process of ordination. One result of this early intensive review is that, once the question of divorce has been examined and set aside, future interviewers are prohibited from making an issue of it for the remainder of the process. This is an example of strong accountability, submission to authority, and, ultimately, a restoration of trust that can open doors for the redemptive work of God through the church and its leaders.

## THOSE WHO FALL AND THEN RISE

To model the ministry of Christ, we must model the patience and compassion that encourages people to accomplish the purposes of God even if they fail in the attempt. We are people of forgiveness, so we are ethically obligated to assist those who fail in a valid attempt at proclaiming the gospel to rise from where they have fallen and move forward in grace. Furthermore, as ambassadors of Christ, we are charged with the responsibility to maintain the integrity of the church in doctrine and practice. This means that those who abuse either the doctrines or the practices of the church (or both) cannot escape correction, regardless of their status or wealth. In addition, the correction we render must leave room for the grace of God to both forgive and, in time, restore those who have fallen. We do, of course, recognize that there are some kinds of moral failure that permanently disqualify a person from ordained ministry. Even so, there is always a place for the fallen to be redeemed, and there is always a place for the redeemed to serve in the kingdom of God.

### Mentoring Questions

1. How does your approach to ministry create an environment of grace in the life of your congregation? Are there specific changes that could make this more of a reality?

2. Is there anything that you need to confess or seek ongoing accountability for?

3. What resources do you know of that could assist those in your congregation following a moral failure?

4. What changes could be made in your congregation to make people more willing to take risks in order to accomplish the church's mission?

5. What safety measures might you implement to protect vulnerable people in your congregation from moral failure?

## Suggested Reading

Beattie, Melody. *Codependent No More.* San Francisco: HarperCollins, 1987.

Earle, Ralph, Jr., and Mark Laaser. *The Pornography Trap.* Kansas City: Beacon Hill Press of Kansas City, 2012.

Laney, J. Carl. *A Guide to Church Discipline.* Eugene, OR: Wipf and Stock, 2010.

Miller, J. Keith. *A Hunger for Healing.* San Francisco: HarperCollins, 1991.

170

# APPENDIX A
## Ministry Resources

A1. Grid for Ethical Decision-Making

A2. Sample Code of Professional Responsibility

A3. Sample Communication Covenant for Ministers and Congregations

A4. Counseling Covenant for Ministers

# A1
## Grid for Ethical Decision-Making

| Theological Quadrant | Priorities Quadrant |
|---|---|
| Discuss the theological rationale behind the decision, keeping in mind sound biblical interpretation based upon the model of Jesus Christ. | Discuss ways in which this decision reflects proper, biblically based priorities for the use of time for those involved. Discuss how this decision and the resources utilized reflect the priorities of the church. |
| **Character Quadrant** | **Relational Quadrant** |
| Discuss how this decision will result in magnifying and pointing to the character of Christ, and how the results of this decision can foster the building of Christlike community in the church and in the world. | Discuss ways in which this decision utilizes ethical communication and promotes an environment of grace, truth, and love among those involved, even if confrontation is necessary. |

# A2

## Sample Code of Professional Responsibility

As a minister of the gospel of Jesus Christ, I am committed to the key theological responsibilities of my calling, which include:

1. Shepherding the flock of God by recognizing that this is God's church and not a possession of mine or anyone else's to be used according to our whims. Rather, we participate together with a spirit of humility and Christ-centered respect for one another. I seek to function as an under-shepherd, carrying out the duties of ministry in keeping with the goals and the methods of the Good Shepherd, Jesus Christ.

2. Being faithful "in season and out of season" by demonstrating consistency in the prioritizing of my time, faithfulness as a disciple of Christ, faithfulness as a spouse and a parent, and faithfulness as a servant-leader of this congregation and community.

3. Preaching the Word in a way that exalts Christ and Christ's ways and not my own sense of importance or control. I will do so without partiality, humbly, and yet without fear, recognizing that I am responsible before God for my faithfulness in proclaiming the message of Christ to this congregation and to the world, and for proclaiming that message in harmony with sound doctrine.

4. Guarding my life and doctrine by being accountable for the way in which I spend my time and my resources, and by maintaining a life of moral purity and consistent growth in the knowledge and application of the doctrine of the church as handed down from Jesus Christ through the writings of Scripture and the leaders of the church.

5. Providing patient and godly counsel to both Christians and non-Christians by developing healthy relationships so as

to be a source of Christ-centered encouragement and loving service through word and deed.

6. Making disciples by first being a disciple myself, availing myself of godly mentors and colleagues whom God can use to make me a better Christian; also by developing relationships with others that point them to Christ, by doing the work of an evangelist, and by speaking the truth in love.

7. Being a person of prayer by setting aside times of individual and family devotions that include consistent interaction with God. Furthermore, I will seek to lead the church in consistent corporate prayer for vision, wisdom, healing, and by making other intercessions on behalf of the people, both in public worship and when offering pastoral care and comfort.

# A3

## Sample Communication Covenant for Ministers and Congregations

As co-laborers together for the purposes of God and God's kingdom through Jesus Christ, empowered by the Holy Spirit, we commit together to the following Communication Covenant.

1. If you have a problem with me, come to me privately.

2. If I have a problem with you, I'll come to you privately.

3. If someone has a problem with me and comes to you, send them to me. I'll do the same for you.

4. If someone consistently will not come to me, say, "Let's go to the pastor together. I am sure he will see us about this." I will do the same for you.

5. Be careful how you interpret me—I'd rather do that. On matters that are unclear, do not feel pressured to interpret my feelings or thoughts. It is easy to misinterpret intentions.

6. I will be careful how I interpret you.

7. If it's confidential, don't tell. This especially applies to board meetings. If you or anyone comes to me in confidence, I won't tell unless (a) the person is going to harm himself or herself, (b) the person is going to physically harm someone else, or (c) a child has been physically or sexually abused. I expect the same from you.

8. I do not read unsigned letters or notes.

9. I do not manipulate; I will not be manipulated; do not let others manipulate you. Do not let others try to manipulate me *through* you. I will not preach "at" you on Sunday mornings. I will leave conviction to the Holy Spirit (he does it better anyway).

10. When in doubt, just say it. The only dumb questions are those that don't get asked. We are a family here and we care about each other, so if you have a concern, pray, and then (if led) speak up. If I can answer it without misrepresenting something or breaking a confidence, I will.

Let us make all of these agreements a matter of consistent prayer and loving accountability so that we may be part of an environment of growth and health in the name of Christ and his kingdom.

# A4
## Counseling Covenant for Ministers

*Given that ministers may have widely varying training and skills in counseling, this agreement is a general outline of the basic points to communicate when entering into a pastoral counseling arrangement. Ministers should feel free to add to or adjust sections of this agreement in ways that are reasonable for their congregation or counseling environment.*

1. *Confidentiality.* I will maintain confidentiality in all matters shared with me in the course of pastoral care. There are exceptions to this pledge, required by pastoral ethics and by law. I will not maintain confidentiality when—

(a) I have reasonable suspicion that the counselee poses an imminent threat to do harm to himself or herself or others. I do, however, recognize the distinction between expressing depressive or even suicidal thoughts and posing an *imminent threat to harm* self or others.

(b) I have received a credible report of the abuse of a minor (for example, physical or sexual abuse) and/or an elderly person.

(c) The counselee(s) agrees in writing that there are matters I can and should share with others.

2. *Limits of Expertise and Availability.* [In this section, describe the extent of your training, your general approach to pastoral counseling, and the limits of your expertise and time available for counseling.]

3. *Referrals.* If I have reason to believe that counselees would benefit from the services of another caregiver, such as a counselor, psychologist, or psychiatrist, I will recommend that they seek such services. I may provide a list of qualified profes-

sionals whom counselees may decide to consult; however, that does not constitute an endorsement of the caregivers or their services.

4. *The Role of the Minister.* As the counseling relationship progresses, the relationship of the minister to the counselee may change due to the changing nature of the care provided. My primary role is to offer biblical wisdom and spiritual support. However, that role may change over time. For example, when a referral to another caregiver is made, when a counselee refuses to accept biblical counsel or sound doctrine, my role may shift to offering secondary support, accountability, or even the termination of the counseling relationship. I pledge to communicate clearly about the nature of this counseling relationship at all times.

# APPENDIX B
## Case Studies

Adapt these case studies in the manner that best suits your situation. I suggest using the Grid for Ethical Decision-Making (Appendix A1) to discuss each aspect of the cases. The key to benefitting from these cases is not necessarily to find one right answer but to work together with mentors, classmates, or others involved in leadership to find a *consistent* answer. That is, to find a solution that is in harmony with both your personal ethics and the ethics of the congregation or denomination in which you serve. Do not be surprised if, over time, you find certain aspects of your solution to these and other case studies change, sometimes in big ways as your understanding and practice of pastoral ethics grows. All of these cases are fictional, but they represent real-life ethical decisions faced by many ministers. Enjoy!

### Case B1: To Move or Not to Move

You are the new pastor of a congregation of about 250 people. The church is located in an impoverished inner-city neighborhood in Detroit. Your congregation has had a long-time presence in the community, but the average income of the fairly affluent members is well above that of the surrounding neighborhood. This is partly because the majority of your congregation—about 65 percent—commute from the suburbs to attend this church. Many of these commuters once lived in the neighborhood but, over the past twenty years or so, have moved out of the city—a case of urban flight. However, they remain committed to this church.

As the new pastor, you are immediately approached by several families in the congregation who are long-range commuters, driving some forty-five minutes to church each week. They ask you to consider relocating to a central suburban location about thirty minutes from the church's current neighborhood. You discover that these families are among your strongest givers, and though they express a strong desire for this church to remain their "home church," they say that they are increasingly uncomfortable commuting to this "dangerous neighborhood" and will therefore consider a change in the next year.

Meanwhile, about 35 percent of the congregation resides within the church's current neighborhood. Of this group, about a third (10 percent or so of the total congregation) are from ethnic groups more representative of the current neighborhood. Some among this group have expressed a desire for the church to be more engaged in the neighborhood—the place they call home.

When you bring this up at the board meeting, after hours of prayer and argument, the board identifies three options:

1. Sell the current building and move to the suggested suburban location. Those who suggest this argue that since a majority of the church is now suburban, this church should become suburban as well. Those in the neighborhood can find churches better suited to their goals, needs, and backgrounds.

2. Stay at the current location and begin a satellite congregation in the suburbs, thereby meeting the needs of all of the backgrounds and ethnicities of the church.

3. Stay at the current location and spend energies and time reaching more deeply into the church's current neighborhood, risking the loss of those who no longer wish to commute.

## Discussion Questions

1. List the positives and negatives of each option.

2. Discuss what you see to be the ethical issues involved, based upon your understanding of the mission of the church (support your ideas with biblical data where possible).

3. Which options may require a more deontological (rule- or principles-based) approach? Which may indicate a more teleological (outcome-centered) approach? Why?

4. What other options might the church take, if any?

5. What would you do and why? Let your answer reflect the reality of consequences that may come.

## Case B2: Confession

"Pastor, I need to meet with you." So began a phone conversation with Dan, one of your most trusted and faithful church members. Later, in your office, Dan begins to cry. "It all started innocently," he begins. "I have known the family for years, and I gave Jane a ride home after a church service two weeks ago. Her husband was away on business, and though I should not have, I went inside for a soda. One thing led to another, and we ended up in a very compromising situation. In the middle of this awkward situation, her husband, Bob, came home early. Fortunately, he remained calm, and we all spent the next few hours talking through the situation together. I left, went home, and we have not mentioned it since. Her husband is disappointed, and he does not want me around them any longer, but he has agreed not to tell anyone, including my wife. She just wouldn't understand, and I want to be sensitive to her feelings. I don't want this to affect my ministry here. I have led music here for years, and I would hate to leave the church in a situation that places more stress on you. I am confessing this to you because I don't want to live with the guilt, and I want to be open to suggestions you have. I'm just confused. Jane and Bob have forgiven me, and I have agreed to have much stricter boundaries in the future. Since they are satisfied with that resolution, do I need to step down from my position of worship leadership? If so, how will I be able to explain this to my wife? Should I tell my wife, or should I just move forward having learned an important lesson about my vulnerabilities? What should we do, Pastor?"

### Discussion Questions

1. What additional information would you need from this church member before making a decision?

2. Should Dan tell his wife? If so, what would be your role? If not, why not?

3. How should this affect Dan's future as a worship leader in the congregation? What steps should be taken now that you know this information?

4. Who would need to be involved in the conversation moving forward? Discuss ways you could approach this next step.

## Case B3: True Story?

You are on staff at a church in a well-to-do suburb. Since you are new, you are getting acquainted with various churches in your district. A colleague of yours in a neighboring suburb invites you to a fund-raiser for missions where you hear a guest missionary who is on furlough. One of the stories he tells seems familiar to you, about a young lady named Anna from a village in southern Africa. As he continues with Anna's story, he displays a black and white photo of a teenage girl labeled "Anna." He speaks in detail about how his family has taken Anna in as part of their family, and that she has been converted to Christianity and is now enjoying educational benefits from the wonderful gifts of people like those in the audience. He closes with a reminder that there are many Annas out there who need our help, and that by giving to missions, we are part of the solution.

The night ends well, and you thank your friend. You cannot stop thinking about the photo of Anna and of the wonderful work the speaker and his family are doing. Then something connects in your memory. You go to your room and pull out a pamphlet from an international Christian ministry that has no relationship with your own denomination or with the guest speaker. As you open the pamphlet, you see it: the same photo the mission speaker shared! The caption reads, "This is Mary, and your gift to Mission International will provide her with food and education for a whole year. There are many Marys out there who need your help. Please give now!"

In your staff meeting the next day, your pastor mentions that he has heard great things about the missions rally at the neighboring church, and that the speaker was very moving. He states that he is considering inviting the same man to speak at an upcoming missions service at your church.

### Discussion Questions

1. Would you tell the colleague who invited you to hear the mission speaker what you discovered in the pamphlet?

2. Would you tell your pastor what you discovered? Would you tell other staff members? Why or why not?

3. What justification might the mission speaker give for using a photo and story that were not his own? How would you analyze a response like this one from the speaker: "Hey, 'Anna' is just a composite of the many kids we see and work with. Putting a face and a name and an actual context (our own family) motivates people to give more to the work of missions so that many more girls and boys can be helped in our work. It doesn't matter that 'Anna' as I described her does not really exist, as long as it helps the overall work, right?"

## Case B4: Nice Doing Business with You

A new roof is needed for the old building that your church meets in. The leaks are becoming noticeable and harder to control. After some preliminary calls to local roofers, you find the average cost for replacing the roof is around $15,000, which would deplete most of your church's savings. A church board member, who is also an independent building contractor, approaches you with the idea of submitting an insurance claim for roof replacement. The only way your insurance will cover the cost is if there is weather-related damage, not normal wear and tear, which is the case with your roof. "Pastor," a member of the building committee says, "we really need this roof or other parts of our church building will be damaged. We did have a bad storm a couple of weeks ago. Who wouldn't believe that storm didn't do some damage to the roof? If we can file a claim with the insurance company, my company will do the job for less than $15,000, and I'll return the extra money back to the church. It will be a win-win!" The chair of the committee looks to you, and says, "Well, Pastor, should we make this our recommendation to the church board?"

### Discussion Questions

    1. What ethical concerns do you have about the proposal?

    2. How would you respond to the board member who made this suggestion?

    3. What alternate approaches would you recommend?

# NOTES

## Introduction: An Ounce of Prevention

1. Note the prevalence of books such as Paul Meier and Frank Minirth, *What They Didn't Teach You in Seminary* (Nashville: Thomas Nelson, 1993).

## Chapter 1: The Art of Ministry Ethics

1. Samuel Wells, *Improvisation: The Drama of Christian Ethics* (Grand Rapids: Brazos Press, 2004).

2. Ibid., 11.

3. Marva Dawn and Eugene Peterson, *The Unnecessary Pastor: Rediscovering the Call* (Grand Rapids: Eerdmans, 2000), 30.

4. Ibid., 31.

5. See Timothy B. Tyson, *Blood Done Sign My Name* (New York: Three Rivers Press, 2004), 318.

6. H. Ray Dunning, *Reflecting the Divine Image: Christian Ethics in Wesleyan Perspective* (Eugene, OR: Wipf and Stock, 2003), 28-29.

7. Jeren Rowell, *Thinking, Listening, Being: A Wesleyan Pastoral Theology* (Kansas City: Beacon Hill Press of Kansas City, 2014), 84.

8. For an introduction to a variety of church structures, see Stephen Cowan, ed., *Who Runs the Church? Four Views on Church Government* (Grand Rapids: Zondervan, 2009).

9. See Dunning, *Reflecting the Divine Image*, 80-81.

10. Paraphrased from Martin Luther King Jr., "23 June 1963—Speech at the Great March on Detroit," Martin Luther King Jr. and the Global Freedom Struggle, http://kingencyclopedia.stanford.edu/encyclopedia/documentsentry/doc_speech_at_the_great_march_on_detroit/index.html (accessed September 2, 2016).

11. For a brief introduction to Kant's approach, see Steve Wilkens, *Beyond Bumper Sticker Ethics: An Introduction to Theories of Right and Wrong* (Downers Grove, IL: InterVarsity Press, 1996), 99-114.

12. For the classic, and some may say most extreme, version of Christian teleological ethics, see Joseph Fletcher, *Situation Ethics: The New Morality* (Philadelphia: Westminster Press, 1966). See also the discussion in J. Philip Wogaman, *Christian Ethics: A Historical Introduction* (Louisville, KY: Westminster John Knox Press, 1993), 86-88.

13. See Dunning, *Reflecting the Divine Image*, 80-81.

14. See Glen Stassen and David Gushee, *Kingdom Ethics* (Downers Grove, IL: InterVarsity Press, 2003), 124.

15. Though different in content, this idea of a grid through which to filter ethical decisions is similar to the approach taken in the field of medical ethics and described in Albert R. Jonsen, Mark Siegler, and William J. Winslade, *Clinical Ethics* (Columbus, OH: McGraw-Hill, 2010).

16. See the late ethicist and theologian Lewis B. Smedes, *The Art of Forgiving* (Nashville: Moorings Press, 1996), 3-12.

17. Eugene Peterson, *The Contemplative Pastor: Returning to the Art of Spiritual Direction* (Grand Rapids: Eerdmans, 1989), 13.

18. Ibid., 15.

## Chapter 2: The Minister as a Professional

1. Gaylord Noyce, *Pastoral Ethics: Professional Responsibilities of the Clergy* (Nashville: Abingdon, 1988), 18.

2. William H. Willimon, *Pastor: The Theology and Practice of Ordained Ministry* (Nashville: Abingdon, 2002), 55-69.

3. Ibid., 70.

4. William F. May, "Images That Shape the Public Obligations of the Pastor," in *Clergy Ethics in a Changing Society*, ed. James P. Wind, et al. (Louisville, KY: Westminster John Knox Press, 1991), 54-83.

5. For a more detailed discussion, see Roderick T. Leupp, *Knowing the Name of God: A Trinitarian Tapestry of Grace, Faith, and Community* (Downers Grove, IL: InterVarsity Press, 1996), 92.

6. Ibid., 95-103.

7. See William A. Dyrness, *Learning about Theology from the Third World* (Grand Rapids: Eerdmans, 1990), 44-45.

## Chapter 3: Critical Relationships in Ministry

1. Barbara Brown Taylor, *Leaving Church: A Memoir of Faith* (San Francisco: HarperCollins, 2006), 98-99.

2. Gregory L. Jones and Kevin R. Armstrong, *Resurrecting Excellence: Shaping Faithful Christian Ministry* (Grand Rapids: Eerdmans, 2006), 115.

3. G. Jeffrey MacDonald, "Sacrificing the Body," *Leadership Journal* (Fall 2015), http://www.christianitytoday.com/le/2015/fall/sacrificing-body .html?paging=off (accessed June 2016).

4. Peterson, *Contemplative Pastor,* 18-19.

5. Alix Christie, *Gutenberg's Apprentice* (San Francisco: HarperCollins, 2014), 94.

6. Immanuel Kant, *Grounding for the Metaphysics of Morals* (1785), trans. James Ellington (Indianapolis: Hackett, 1993), 36-37.

7. Eugene Peterson, "Introduction," *Practice Resurrection: A Conversation on Growing up in Christ* (Grand Rapids: Eerdmans, 2010), 1-10.

8. Will D. Campbell, *Brother to a Dragonfly* (New York: Continuum, 1977), 75.

9. Reinhold Niebuhr, *Leaves from the Notebook of a Tamed Cynic* (Louisville, KY: Westminster John Knox Press, 1980), 31.

10. Ibid., 32.

11. Ibid., 18. This is from an entry made in 1917 in this highlighted journal.

## Chapter 4: Communication, the Lifeblood of Ministry

1. See Appendix A for a reproducible version of this Communication Covenant. Originally published as Charles W. Christian, "Ten Rules of Respect," *Leadership Journal* 20, no. 3 (Summer 1999): 55.

2. See, for example, John Maxwell, *There's No Such Thing as "Business" Ethics* (New York: Hachette Book Group, 2003), 4-5.

3. Martin Luther King Jr., *Stride toward Freedom: The Montgomery Story* (1958; repr., Boston: Beacon Press, 2010), 39, Amazon.com, https://www .amazon.com/Stride-Toward-Freedom-Montgomery-Legacy-ebook/dp /B009U9S54K/ref=sr_1_1?s=books&ie=UTF8&qid=1473182442&sr=1-1& keywords=stride+toward+freedom#reader_B009U9S54K.

4. I write about this in "The Ethics of Preaching: Some Things to Keep in Mind," *Preacher's Magazine* (Pentecost 2005): 48-52.

5. Ronald W. Richardson, *Creating a Healthier Church* (Minneapolis: Augsburg Fortress Press, 1996), 115.

6. Ibid., 116.

7. See Thom S. Rainier, "Nine Traits of Church Bullies," *ThomRainier. com* (blog), http://thomrainer.com/2015/03/nine-traits-church-bullies/ (accessed December 2015).

8. For more information about clear online communication, there are several handy etiquette guides online. See also Rena Palloff and Keith

Pratt, *Building Learning Communities in Cyberspace: Effective Strategies for the Online Classroom* (San Francisco: Jossey-Bass, 1999).

## Chapter 5: Dealing with Church Conflicts

1. See Les Carter and Frank Minirth, *The Anger Workbook* (Nashville: Thomas Nelson, 1993), 23-24.

2. Ibid., 92-93.

## Chapter 6: The Ethics of Pastoral Care and Counseling

1. Thomas C. Oden, *Pastoral Theology: Essentials of Ministry* (New York: HarperCollins, 1983), 49-50.

2. Ibid., 52.

3. Larry Crabb, *Connecting: Healing for Ourselves and Our Relationships* (Nashville: Word Publishing, 1997), xx.

4. See a recent article on ministry malpractice: Richard R. Hammar, "Pastoral Liability—Malpractice," *Church Law and Tax*, June 5, 2015, http://www.churchlawandtax.com/lessons/content/pastoral-liabilitymalpractice.html (accessed December 2015).

5. Howard W. Stone, "A Case for Brief Pastoral Counseling," in *Strategies for Brief Pastoral Counseling*, ed. Howard W. Stone (Minneapolis: Augsburg Fortress Press, 2001), 3-22.

6. Ibid., 14-15.

7. Special thanks to attorney Michael Thompson, lead counsel for the Church of the Nazarene, for a helpful conversation about the legal and ethical boundaries of sharing confidences as a minister.

8. See Billy Graham, *Just As I Am: The Autobiography of Billy Graham* (New York: HarperCollins, 2011), 651.

9. Special thanks to Edna Christian, Rev. Deanna Hayden, Dr. Carla Sunberg, Dr. Vicki Copp, and Dr. Judi Schwanz for conversing with me in more detail on this matter.

10. T. Scott Daniels, *The First 100 Days* (Kansas City: Beacon Hill Press of Kansas City, 2011), 136.

## Chapter 7: Handling the Business of Ministry

1. Alexander Hill, *Just Business: Christian Ethics for the Marketplace* (Downers Grove, IL: InterVarsity Press, 2008), 69-70.

2. J. Clif Christopher, *Not Your Parents' Offering Plate: A New Vision for Financial Stewardship* (Nashville: Abingdon Press, 2008), 13-14.

3. Gary L. McIntosh and Charles Arn, *What Every Pastor Should Know: 101 Indispensable Rules of Thumb for Leading Your Church* (Grand Rapids: Baker Books, 2013), 208.

4. Ibid., 33. The title of the chapter is "All Members Are Not Equal."

5. See ibid., 39-40.

6. Ibid., 40.

7. Ibid., 35.

8. See Matthew 13 for the parable of the sower. I owe this thought on the "inefficiency" of Jesus to many sermons I have heard from gifted preachers through the years, most recently in a sermon by William Willimon.

9. See Nina Eliasoph, "Introduction," *The Politics of Volunteering* (London: Polity Press, 2013), 1-8.

10. For a summary of this case against International Church of the Foursquare Gospel local denominational officials in Oregon, see Andrew Scroggin, "Oregon Appeals Court Backs Former Veronia Pastor," *Oregonian*, February 8, 2010, http://www.oregonlive.com/news/index.ssf/2010/02/oregon_appeals_court_backs_pas.html (accessed August 8, 2016); see commentary on this case by attorney Richard Hammar: "Oregon Case Provides a Powerful Reminder to Churches," Managing Your Church, *Church Law and Tax*, February 17, 2010, http://www.churchlawandtax.com/blog/2010/february/oregon-case-provides-powerful-reminder-to-churches.html (accessed December 2015).

## Chapter 8: Ethical Worship and Preaching

1. See Robert L. Webber, ed., *Twenty Centuries of Christian Worship*, The Complete Library of Christian Worship (Peabody, MA: Hendrickson, 1994), 2:84-86.

2. Ibid.

3. See Elmer Towns and Vernon Whaley, *Worship through the Ages* (Nashville: Broadman and Holman, 1995), 293-95.

4. See such recent contributions as Robert E. Webber, *Ancient-Future Worship* (Grand Rapids: Baker Books, 2008); and D. H. Williams, *Evangelicals and Tradition* (Grand Rapids: Baker Books, 2005).

5. See Stanley Hauerwas and William H. Willimon, *Resident Aliens: Life in the Christian Colony* (Nashville: Abingdon Press, 1989), 123.

6. Ibid., 138.

7. See Jeremy Begbie, ed., *Behold the Glory: Incarnation Through the Arts* (Grand Rapids: Baker Books, 2000), 146-47.

8. Williams, *Evangelicals and Tradition*, 24-25.

9. Rob Staples, *Outward Sign, Inward Grace: The Place of Sacraments in Wesleyan Spirituality* (Kansas City: Beacon Hill Press of Kansas City, 1991), 63.

10. Ibid.

11. An overview may be found in a variety of systematic theologies, as well as monographs such as Staples, *Outward Sign, Inward Grace*, 85-118. Also, see Brent Peterson, *Created to Worship* (Kansas City: Beacon Hill Press of Kansas City, 2012), 151-83. A classic work on the subject of the sacraments is John Macquarrie's book titled *A Guide to the Sacraments* (New York: Continuum, 1997), 101-56. In Macquarrie's book, chapters 10–14 address the Eucharist.

12. For more detail, see Peterson, *Created to Worship*, 181.

13. See Macquarrie, *Guide to the Sacraments*, 22, where Macquarrie laments the separation of Word and Sacrament, seeing each as a complement of the other.

14. See Tony Campolo, *Let Me Tell You a Story: Life Lessons from Unexpected Places and Unlikely People* (Nashville: Thomas Nelson, 2000), 30-31.

15. Ibid.

16. Ibid.

17. Peterson, *Created to Worship*, 199.

18. Gilbert VanDooren, *The Beauty of Reformed Liturgy* (Winnipeg: Premier Printing, 1980), 48.

19. See McGraw, "Benediction in Corporate Worship," 15.

20. Thomas G. Long, *Accompany Them with Singing: The Christian Funeral* (Louisville, KY: Westminster John Knox Press, 2009), 5.

21. Ibid., 7.

22. Ibid.

23. William H. Willimon, *Peculiar Speech: Preaching to the Baptized* (Grand Rapids: Eerdmans, 1992).

24. Ibid., 12.

25. Justo and Catherine Gonzalez, *Liberation Preaching: The Pulpit and the Oppressed* (Nashville: Abingdon Press, 1980), 39.

26. See Willimon, *Peculiar Speech*, 12.

## Chapter 9: Failing, Falling, and the Ethics of Grace

1. Chuck Swindoll, *The Grace Awakening* (Nashville: Word Books, 1989), 133-34.

2. Daniel Brown with Brian Larson, *The Other Side of Pastoral Ministry* (Grand Rapids: Zondervan, 1996), 151-52.

3. L. Gregory Jones and Kevin R. Armstrong, *Resurrecting Excellence* (Grand Rapids: Eerdmans, 2006), 27.

4. Brown, *The Other Side of Pastoral Ministry*, 154-55.

5. See Appendix A1, "Grid for Ethical Decision-Making."

6. J. Keith Miller, *A Hunger for Healing* (San Francisco: HarperCollins, 1991), 4.

7. See Melody Beattie, *Codependent No More* (San Francisco: Harper-Collins, 1987), 30-31.